Ting Zhang

AGING IN THE "KNOWLEDGE ECONOMY"

Ting Zhang

AGING IN THE "KNOWLEDGE ECONOMY":

CRISES OR OPPORTUNITIES?

VDM Verlag Dr. Müller

Impressum/Imprint (nur für Deutschland/ only for Germany)
Bibliografische Information der Deutschen Nationalbibliothek: Die Deutsche Nationalbibliothek
verzeichnet diese Publikation in der Deutschen Nationalbibliografie; detaillierte bibliografische
Daten sind im Internet über http://dnb.d-nb.de abrufbar.
Alle in diesem Buch genannten Marken und Produktnamen unterliegen warenzeichen-, marken-
oder patentrechtlichem Schutz bzw. sind Warenzeichen oder eingetragene Warenzeichen der
jeweiligen Inhaber. Die Wiedergabe von Marken, Produktnamen, Gebrauchsnamen,
Handelsnamen, Warenbezeichnungen u.s.w. in diesem Werk berechtigt auch ohne besondere
Kennzeichnung nicht zu der Annahme, dass solche Namen im Sinne der Warenzeichen- und
Markenschutzgesetzgebung als frei zu betrachten wären und daher von jedermann benutzt
werden dürften.

Coverbild: www.purestockx.com

Verlag: VDM Verlag Dr. Müller Aktiengesellschaft & Co. KG
Dudweiler Landstr. 125 a, 66123 Saarbrücken, Deutschland
Telefon +49 681 9100-698, Telefax +49 681 9100-988, Email: info@vdm-verlag.de

Herstellung in Deutschland:
Schaltungsdienst Lange o.H.G., Zehrensdorfer Str. 11, D-12277 Berlin
Books on Demand GmbH, Gutenbergring 53, D-22848 Norderstedt
Reha GmbH, Dudweiler Landstr. 99, D- 66123 Saarbrücken
ISBN: 978-3-639-07612-7

Imprint (only for USA, GB)
Bibliographic information published by the Deutsche Nationalbibliothek: The Deutsche
Nationalbibliothek lists this publication in the Deutsche Nationalbibliografie; detailed
bibliographic data are available in the Internet at http://dnb.d-nb.de.
Any brand names and product names mentioned in this book are subject to trademark, brand or
patent protection and are trademarks or registered trademarks of their respective holders. The
use of brand names, product names, common names, trade names, product descriptions etc.
even without
a particular marking in this works is in no way to be construed to mean that such names may be
regarded as unrestricted in respect of trademark and brand protection legislation and could thus
be used by anyone.

Cover image: www.purestockx.com

Publisher:
VDM Verlag Dr. Müller Aktiengesellschaft & Co. KG
Dudweiler Landstr. 125 a, 66123 Saarbrücken, Germany
Phone +49 681 9100-698, Fax +49 681 9100-988, Email: info@vdm-verlag.de

Copyright © 2008 VDM Verlag Dr. Müller Aktiengesellschaft & Co. KG and licensors
All rights reserved. Saarbrücken 2008

Produced in USA and UK by:
Lightning Source Inc., 1246 Heil Quaker Blvd., La Vergne, TN 37086, USA
Lightning Source UK Ltd., Chapter House, Pitfield, Kiln Farm, Milton Keynes, MK11 3LW, GB
BookSurge, 7290 B. Investment Drive, North Charleston, SC 29418, USA
ISBN: 978-3-639-07612-7

DEDICATION

Aiyu Yu (1948-2008), the Author's Mother

This book is first of all dedicated to my mother, Aiyu Yu, who was fighting against extreme cancer pain until the last moment of her life and whose wisdom, courage, and persistence encouraged me throughout this entire adventure. It is also dedicated to my father, Hongfa Zhang, and my mother's two sisters, Jieyu Yu and Chanyu Yu, who have tried their best with all possible efforts, patience, and sacrifice to save my mother's life and accompany her for the precious last period of life.

Acknowledgement

I am deeply indebted to my advisor and mentor Prof. Laurie Schintler, who has been extremely resourceful, patient and approachable throughout the course of my book writing. I am also indebted to Prof. Roger Stough, Prof. David Wong, and Prof. Zoltan Acs from George Mason University whose help, provoking suggestions and encouragement helped me throughout my study of this Ph.D. program and my research on seniors, entrepreneurship, and regional economics. I would also like to thank my external reader Prof. Maryann Feldman from University of Georgia whose encouragement and inspiration made this book more possible.

I want to thank the School of Public Policy at George Mason University for providing me important knowledge and skills to start and finish this book project. I have particular thanks to faculty members of the School of Public Policy for offering me sustainable financial, knowledge, and network support to finish this book. Among them, I am particularly obliged to Prof. Naoru Koizumi, Prof. Jeremy Mayer, Prof. Kingsley Haynes, Prof. Jean Paelinck, Prof. Stephen Fuller, Prof. Stephen Ruth, Prof. David Hart, and Prof. Ann Baker. Prof. Richard Florida has helped me understand his concept of "creative class" and with data on Social Tolerance Index. My further thank would be expressed to Dr. Jules Lichtenstein from the AARP whose interests in my research encouraged me.

My colleagues from the School of Public Policy of George Mason University supported me in my research work. I want to thank them for all their help, support, interest and valuable suggestions. Especially I am obliged to Lisa Fowler, Chunpu Song, Adriana Kocornik-Mina, Shaoming Cheng, Lei Ding, Qingshu Xie, Henry Vega, and Huaqun Li. I also want to thank Mr. Raj Kulkarni for all his assistance on the GIS. My sister, Qun Zhang looked closely at the final version of the book for English style and grammar, correcting both and offering suggestions for improvement.

Finally, I would like to give my special thanks to my husband Gary Armstrong whose patient love enabled me to complete this work.

Table of Contents

List of Figures and Tables

List of Abbreviations

AARP   :   American Association of Retired Persons
ATIS   :   Advanced Traveler Information System
ARITMS :   Advanced Regional Traffic Interactive Management and Information System
BLS   :   Bureau of Labor Statistics
CBR   :   Crude Birth Rate
CED   :   Committee for Economic Development
DR   :   Dependency Ratio
EDR   :   Elderly Dependency Ratio
ERIPS   :   Early Retirement Incentive Programs
ESPON   :   European Spatial Planning Observation Network
FIRE   :   Finance, Insurance, and Real Estate
GDP   :   Gross Domestic Product
GEM   :   Global Entrepreneurship Monitor
GIS   :   Geographic Information System
HR   :   Human Resources
HRS   :   Health and Retirement Study
ICT   :   Information and Communication Technologies
LM   :   Lagrange Multiplier
LQ   :   Location Quotients
OASDI   :   Old age, Survivors, and Disability Insurance
OECD   :   Organization for Economic Co-operation and Development
OLS   :   Ordinary Least Square
MSAs   :   Metropolitan Statistical Areas

11

NAICS	:	North America Industry Classification System
NCOE	:	U.S. National Commission on Entrepreneurship
NOWCC	:	National Older Worker Career Center
NPTS	:	Nationwide Personal Transportation Survey
NSF	:	National Science Foundation
PMSAs	:	Primary Metropolitan Statistical Areas
PUMA	:	Public Use Microdata Sample Areas
PUMS	:	Public Use Microdata Samples
RHS	:	Retirement History Surveys
R&D	:	Research and Development
SHRM	:	Society for Human Resource Management
SIC	:	Standard Industrial Classification
SOC	:	Standard Occupation Classification codes
SSA	:	Social Security Administration
SSB	:	Social Security Bureau
TEA	:	Total Entrepreneurial Activity

Part I Introduction

The population is aging, not only just in developed countries; it also occurs to many developing countries. Aging, to a large extent, brings the society a sort of fear: how can the economy cope with the increasingly large retiree cohorts, how can the future young people produce enough social products and service to guarantee seniors' welfare, how can the government pay for future seniors' retirement, how would the future Social Security system go, and how could fiscal budget balance well between revenue, policy practice, and overwhelming seniors' health care and financial demands? Those are the questions many people concern. Following this mind set, aging implies crises and seniors implies social burden.

Seniors, at least most of them, have contributed their heart and soul to the society's progress and prosperity. Do they just deserve being considered unwanted burden and being stereotyped as obsolete, slow, unproductive, etc? We all have our senior years. Do we like to face a gloomy late life that is lack of deserving social respect after accumulating many years' experience and skills? Of course not!

In many cultures, seniors are instead highly respected and perceived to be wiser than the young and seniors have traditionally been the decision maker, the leader of a family and community, the authority of knowledge and information, and the power of the society. In those societies, seniors are well taken care of, either by their own offspring and family, or by various government and social programs. In the United States, the political chiefs and leaders at various levels are seniors; however, seniors are not necessary well respected everywhere and there seems to exist a certain level of old-age discrimination and negative images of being old. With the growing older population and relatively shrinking younger population, even in the traditionally senior friendly societies, seniors, as a major group of consumers and to a much less extent as producers, would bring in increasing worries, concerns, and even crises.

Is aging destined to bring about crises? If demography is really the destiny of our socioeconomic development, aging does not necessarily mean just crises. Instead, why cannot seniors be treated in a more positive way? Seniors, with many years' cumulative job skills, social ties, and various other virtues, such as years' of experience assets, mature business ties, outstanding language skills, mentorship and guidance, can be extremely valuable to the economic and social development. As long as their health allows, they can still be highly active

14

in the socioeconomic activities, and in many cases, can play even a better leading role than the younger ones.

Message of this Book

When we recall the history, seniors do not retire as early as 62 that is the current average retirement age in the United States. Decades ago, it is not unusual at all for seniors to work until mid 70s. Let alone most jobs back then are much more labor intensive than jobs we are facing now. We are currently in the "Knowledge Economy" in which knowledge, thinking, skills are the key factors driving economic growth. If seniors of decades ago could even work until 70s for heavy industrial physical labor work, why cannot current seniors work longer and stay productive and valuable until 70s and even later? With better nutrition and health conditions, working until 70s or later is not physically impossible for many seniors, as long as seniors would like to do so.

However, please note that the author is NOT purporting forcing seniors to continuing working and stay in the labor force while they really want to retire. Part of the message this book delivers is to ensure a motivating and supportive environment for seniors to continue being active in socioeconomic society and give seniors who want to continue working decent career opportunities and a welcoming job market.

Many seniors, after years of working experience building a career, do not really want to retire in 60s. They love their career and would like to keep contributing their energy and wisdom to the society and would like to continue enjoying the career they have been loving for decades. However, the pension penalty, some continued early retirement incentives, other unfriendly and even implicitly discriminative social elements, and seniors' own needs to take care of other family members hinder them from continuing to pursue their career ambitions and enjoyments. Difficult bosses, unfriendly working environments, and any small unpleasant factor can easily deter seniors from continue participating in the labor force, if the atmosphere of seniors' occupational freedom is not built.

There is a concern about seniors' obsolete skills. However, the situation of obsolete skills is socially constructed. Details of this will be explained in later chapters. If seniors did not stay away from the labor market for too long, they would not face obsolete skills. Age is not necessarily a deterministic factor for skill obsolesce, but serious isolation from socioeconomic actives can be. Seniors can still learn. We all see seniors in graduate schools and they perform well. We also see grandparents learn various skills they are interested in. As long as physical and mentally health does not totally fail, there is no sufficient evidence that seniors cannot learn.

For those seniors who wish to retire and do not want to continue working, it is first of all their personal choice and individuals' rights to choose working or retiring. On the other hand, if an elderly friendly working environment is mature, many seniors may possibly still be interested in continue working. Many established seniors like to have their own long vacation, like to spend time with grandchildren and other family members and friends, and like to travel around. In this case, certain level of flexibility allowing for time freedom to arrange individuals' working schedules would be an extremely helpful approach to accommodate seniors' labor force participation. Phased retirement is an option that considers both freedom of retirement life and fun of working. In this case, job performance evaluation based on final products and services rather than working time would possibly be a better measure. Additionally, for those seniors who are eager to retire, they are most likely not to have had a career they could enjoy or have been working in unpleasant situation for a long time. People have the natural need for self-actualization. If a pleasant environment is provided, many seniors would possibly choose to continue working, instead of suffer from boredom of staying home.

Seniors, though physically perceived to be less vigorous than the younger ones, have their own unique comparative advantages for career pursuits, particularly in the "Knowledge Economy". Aging does not necessarily only mean challenges to the society; it also offers tremendous opportunities to the economy and society, if seniors' mental assets are appreciated and utilized well. Seniors, in the knowledge-, skill-, and wisdom-based economy, can not only directly become part of the labor force, they can also become entrepreneurs, innovating and creating more jobs, and offer guidance to the young. This would not only directly contribute to the economy, but also can largely mitigate the prognostic fiscal and labor crises that the aging population is predicted to result in. Therefore, aging can be the opportunities to achieve new incredible socio-economic growth, with smart social and policy directions. This is the message this book attempts to deliver.

Key Definitions in this Book

This book defines several terms; the most important two are "seniors" and "Knowledge Economy". The definition of the term *seniors, older people, or the elderly*, depends on the situations. As long as data is available, this book measures older people and seniors as people who are aged 62 and above. The reason for this definition is two folded. First, 62 is the initial eligibility of Social Security; Second, the U.S. working people's average retirement age is 62 (Gendell, 2001). Since this book address seniors' occupational choices, people who are older than retirement age would be the key group under this research.

On the other hand, data for seniors who are aged at or above 62 is often unavailable. Most aging research and publicly available data uses the cutoff point at age 65 to define seniors. Most datasets and literature define seniors as who are aged 65 or older. There are a few occasional cases that seniors are actually defined as those who are 55 or older. In this book, the majority age data is from the Public Use Micro Sample (PUMS) data, in which detailed age data is available and therefore the ideal cutoff point 62 is applied. The rule of thumb in this book's definition of seniors is as follows: when using PUMS data for empirical tests, seniors are defined as of age 62 or above; all other empirical analyses use 65 as the cutoff point; when previous studies are cited, the definitions of seniors and older people follow what the literature offered, i.e. either those who aged 65 and above or those who aged 55 and above.

The second key term is *"Knowledge Economy"*. The simple explanation of the "Knowledge Economy" is a knowledge and human capital based economy. It is in the knowledge-based economic context that seniors' labor force participation and elderly entrepreneurship becomes more possible and especially valuable. The knowledge base relies on human capital and the "Knowledge Economy" is less physically demanding. The reliance on human capital instead of physical labor in the "Knowledge Economy" makes it more possible for seniors to stay in the labor force and makes seniors' cumulated insights, skills, and business ties particularly valuable.

The scale or size of the "Knowledge Economy" (or knowledge-base sectors) is defined by the "creative class" employment that is addressed in Florida (2004)[1]. The term "creative class" has a clear occupational classification[2] and delineates creativity, knowledge base, and innovation. Reich (1992), a previous attempt to describe the "Knowledge Economy", defined those in the knowledge-based occupations as "symbolic analysts". Symbolic analysts solve, identify, or broker problems by manipulating symbols or abstract images using analytical tools (such as mathematics, financial gimmicks, and legal arguments). Eventually, the work of the symbolic analysts transforms the symbols into products and services or, thus, reality. Reich's concept is interesting, but he did not offer a clear operational definition with a classification of occupations. Florida (2004) addressed this concern and provided a definition for the "creative class" under the U.S. Standard Occupation Classification codes (SOC). The creative class jobs include knowledge-intensive jobs, such as scientist, engineers, and other professional occupations. Although Florida's creative class was intended to address human creativity[3], his classification is conceptually similar to Reich's characterization of knowledge-based occupations. Florida observed that creativity is becoming more valuable in today's global

---

[1] It is necessary to note that this book only uses Florida (2004)'s occupation classification for Creative Class, which differs from his Creativity Index or Global Creativity Index. His Creativity Index (see Florida 2004) is a composite measure that is based on four indices: the Innovation Index, High-Tech Index, Gay Index, and the Creative Class. His Global Creativity Index (see Florida 2005) is composed of an equally weighted combination of the Talent Index, Technology Index, and the Tolerance Index.

[2] Those occupations include management, business and financial operation, computer and mathematical, architecture and engineering, science, legal, education, arts and media, health care practitioners, and high level sales management occupations.

[3] Among his creative class, Florida (2004) further distinguished Super-Creative Core from other Creative Professionals. Arts, design, entertainment, sports, and media occupations are included in the Super-Creative Core; the Super-Creative Core is argued to be more creative and contributive to the economy than Creative Professionals. This book does not focus on this interpretation of creativity by Florida (2004), but his occupational classification for the Creative Class in general fits the purpose of defining knowledge-based occupations in this book.

economy and finds that the creative class comprises about 30% to 40% of the current U.S. labor force. Within the last decade, this segment of the labor force has increased a great deal.

Methodology and Data

This book's methodology includes interpretive analysis, descriptive statistics, empirical hypotheses testing using statistical modeling, and a case study. The empirical testing method uses a logit model, an extended growth model, and a path analysis model. Location quotients are also used to compare regional industrial concentrations. Spatial econometric modeling and mapping are also used in this book. The methodologies used in individual chapters are contingent to the data availability.

The analysis draws on several streams of theories, including demographic theories, economic growth theories, social gerontology theories, and entrepreneurship theories. Each stream of the above theories is weaved into the analysis. The demographic theories and concepts are used to interpret the long-term aging trend of the U.S. society. The economic growth theories offer a theoretical framework for the existence of the "Knowledge Economy" and for analysis and empirical tests on the economic impact of elderly entrepreneurship. The social gerontology theories are cited to address the concern whether seniors are supposed to continue to active in socioeconomic life. The entrepreneurship theories not only help to explain its association with the "Knowledge Economy", but also interpret seniors' occupational choice.

Most data come from the U.S. Census Bureau, including data from the U.S. Census population estimates, the Census Public Use Micro Sample (PUMS), and the census Local Employment Dynamics (or *Profiles of Older Workers*). Other data sources include Bureau of Economic Analysis and Bureau of Labor Statistics, Social Security Administration, and American Community Survey.

Road Map of this Book

By interpreting several major demographic and economic theories and literature, this book first introduces the concept of the "Knowledge Economy" in the next part, Part II, and analyzes the implications of aging in Part III. To delineate further what kind of unique opportunities the "Knowledge Economy" could bring, not only the economic growth drives are compared to the precedent "Fordist Economy", but the traditional core-periphery regional economic structure is challenged in Part II. Part III first analyzes aging as a long-term demographic trend in the human history and thus indicates the long-run importance of finding solutions to the aging related potential crises. Then, this part interprets in detail the potential labor shortage and fiscal crisis that aging could bring about.

After setting the economic and demographic backgrounds in Part II and III, Part IV first summarizes the personal and social possibilities and necessities for seniors to participate in the labor force and further argues that the "Knowledge Economy" can offer special career, job, and life opportunities to seniors. Later on, this part addresses senior workers' industry preferences and then seniors' employability and occupational choice with empirical evidence. This part identifies entrepreneurship as a unique occupational choice for seniors in the "Knowledge Economy".

Part V addresses the dynamic interaction between seniors and the "Knowledge Economy". To investigate seniors' impact on the "Knowledge Economy", empirical tests on the regional economic, labor, and fiscal impact of elderly entrepreneurship are first conducted. Then a case study addressing the impact of the "Knowledge Economy" on seniors' life is situated at the end of the book through analyzing the potentials of the advanced traveler information technology to serve seniors' travel needs. This book finally concludes with major findings and policy implications.

Part II "Knowledge Economy"

Chapter 1 "Knowledge Economy" in Growth Theories[4]

When addressing whether the demographic phenomenon, aging, brings about crises or opportunity, a crucial economic background cannot be ignored—the "Knowledge Economy". It is in the economic setting of the "Knowledge Economy", aging brings about potential opportunities and hope to mitigate the aging related labor and fiscal crises. Therefore, this book starts with describing the "Knowledge Economy".

1.1 What is the "Knowledge Economy"?

The "Knowledge Economy" is different from the "Fordist economy" in that it is driven by knowledge and innovation rather than just capital and labor (see Table 1.1). Due to the diffusion of information technology, "footloose" information technology organizes business structures in a horizontal network that annihilates space differences, and thus many businesses have successfully outsourced engineering, accounting, etc. (Jarboe and Alliance, 2001). In the "Knowledge Economy", knowledge stock through education, training, and social network is increasingly important; the traditional skills required for the workplace are being replaced by strong academic skills, thinking, reasoning, teamwork skills, and proficiency of using technology (21st Century Labor force Commission, 2000). Earning power is thus highly associated with education attainment, working experience, and interpersonal skills, as seen in job requirements. Because of the importance of knowledge and innovation in the "Knowledge Economy", service

---

[4] Part of the literature review in this chapter is excerpted from Zhang (2008).

industries become increasingly critical in the U.S. economy; traditional sectors, such as manufacturing, mining, and agriculture, are shrinking. Knowledge workers[5] play a more and more important role in the U.S. economy (Reich, 1992). As an evidence of a transition to the "Knowledge Economy", the original Standard Industrial Classification (SIC) code was recently replaced with the new North American Industry Classification System (NAICS) code that includes categories for the sectors that define the "Knowledge Economy". The progress in the economic theories that explain growth reflects this transformation from the "Fordist economy" to the "Knowledge Economy". The next section therefore introduces the development of economic growth theories.

Table 1.1 the "Knowledge Economy" vs. the "Fordist Economy"

Attributes for comparison	"Fordist Economy" (old)	"Knowledge Economy" (new)
Economy-wide Characteristics		
Organizational Form	Vertically integrated	Horizontally integrated
Production characteristics		
Growth driver	Material resources: capital and labor	Innovation, invention and knowledge
Role of research and innovation in the economy	Low moderate	High
Infrastructure characteristics		
Form	Hard (physical)	Soft (information and organizations)
Transport	Miles of highway	Travel time reduction via IT
Learning	Talking head, a skill or degree	Distance learning, lifelong learning

Source: Adapted from Atkinson and Court 1998; Jin and Stough 1998; Zhang (2008).

---

[5] People whose jobs are based on knowledge, or knowledge-driven.

23

The characteristics of the "Knowledge Economy" offer more professional opportunities to the elderly than the "Fordist economy" could. As indicated earlier, in the "Knowledge Economy", human capital, which is characterized by such factors as experience, information, skills, education attainment, social network, and health (Becker, 1986, 1992, 1990, and 1993), has become a central element for economic growth in the "Knowledge Economy". Seniors possess many of these above characteristics with accumulated working experience, management skills, mentoring skills, a mature social network, and job-specific skills.

In the "Knowledge Economy", the types of jobs are not as physically demanding as in the more manufacturing based "Fordist economy". This situation makes it possible for seniors to be more involved in the labor force. The "footloose" characteristic facilitated by the information technology reduces the constraints of location and requirement of mobility, which makes the "Knowledge Economy" more elderly friendly and further enhance older people's human capital in the "Knowledge Economy".

1.2 "Knowledge Economy" in Growth Theories

Economists have attempted to interpret the factors that drive growth. The neoclassic growth models use physical capital and labor to explain the factors that through scale economies drive growth. These models are insufficient to fully explain economic growth in the "Knowledge Economy". As Cicone and Hall (1996) indicated, physical capital accumulation can only explain a small amount of the variation in economic growth across regions in the "Knowledge Economy". Economists therefore have begun to explore better models to interpret the economic growth and to incorporate new growth drivers in the "Knowledge Economy".

1.2.1 Neoclassical Growth Theory

The neoclassical growth theory is the most prevalent and widely accepted growth theory. Based on the basic production function[6] that assumes a diminishing marginal product of capital, physical capital stock and labor are viewed as the two drivers of economic growth for the neoclassical growth theory. Using the national income accounts identity for a closed economy, Solow (1957) argues that the economy ends up with a steady-state level of capital[7] because investment raises capital stock but depreciation reduces it.

The Solow model later generates a few extensions. The extended Solow models recognize the positive impact of population growth on the capital stock, but predict that higher population growth will generate lower levels of GDP per person. Support for this prediction was found by Barro and Sala-i-Martin (1995) and Barro and Lee (1994). Although technology was included as an economic growth driver in the analysis, neoclassical economists assumed technology to be an exogenous variable and the only factor that contributes to persistently rising living standards (Mankiw, 2005).

Technology is treated as an exogenous variable for the neoclassic growth theory and knowledge is not integrated into the Solow model. The neoclassic growth theory emphasizes the role of two inputs—physical capital and labor—in production, but the economic growth predicted by the Solow models typically falls short of the actual growth observed. This is particularly so in the "knowledge-based economy". This difference between the predicted and observed growth is referred to as the "Solow residual". Although the extended Solow models

---

[6] This production function states that output Y depends on the capital stock K and the labor force L, $Y= f(K, L)$.

[7] When the economy starts with less than the steady-state level of capital, the level of investment exceeds the amount of depreciation, and the capital stock will rise with output until it reaches the steady state; when the economy starts with the capital above the steady-state level, investment is less than depreciation, and the capital stock will fall to the steady-state level. The steady state represents the long-run equilibrium of the economy where investment equals depreciation, and there is no pressure for the capital stock to either increase or decrease (Mankiw, 2005).

incorporate the role of technology, they do not explain how the technology is generated and they only treat technology as an exogenous factor. Given the importance of technology and knowledge in the "Knowledge Economy", neoclassical models do not well incorporate the new elements of the "Knowledge Economy".

1.2.2 Endogenous Growth Theory

Endogenous growth theory highlights the role of knowledge and technology. This theory considers knowledge and technological change[8] to be endogenous factors[9], similar to labor and capital, for the long-run steady state growth in a closed economy. By incorporating knowledge and technology as endogenous factors, the new growth theory accounts for a portion of the "Solow residual" that was the unexplained growth in the Solow model and thus explains more of the variation in economic growth than the neoclassic growth models. The endogenous growth theory also starts with a production function[10], but this function does not assume diminishing returns to capital and labor. While physical capital exhibits the property of diminishing returns, knowledge, treated as a type of capital, does not possess the property of diminishing returns. The new growth theory claims that knowledge is a non-rival, non-excludable, intangible, and reusable good with the marginal cost of production near zero (Romer 1993, 1994; Mankiw 2005). Further revisions add that knowledge is not always a non-rival and non-exclusive. The exceptions that generate this revision are patents, trademarks, and copyrights.

Endogenous growth theory better explains long-run sustained regional economic growth in the high-value added "Knowledge Economy" and helps to reveal the positive (or partially positive[11]) externalities and spillover effects of knowledge capital. The new growth theory treats

---

[8] That is based on knowledge, skills, or human capital.

[9] Because technology is treated as an endogenous variable, the new growth theory is also called "endogenous growth theory".

[10] $Y = AK$, where Y is output, K is the capital stock, and A is a constant measuring the amount of output produced for each unit of capital.

[11] Though sometimes the positive externality is challenged because of enhanced exclusiveness of knowledge capital through patent, trademarks, and copyrights.

knowledge as (sometimes partially) non-rival and non-excludable[12]. This newer theory also posits that knowledge spillovers are an important mechanism underlying endogenous growth (Romer, 1986; Lucas, 1988; and Grossman and Helpman, 1991).

However, this theory does not interpret how knowledge spills over and assumes that knowledge spillovers are automatic, costless, and unconstrained by spatial factors. In reality, knowledge does not automatically spill over; instead, knowledge spillovers are costly, and geographically constrained (Acs et al., 2004). This unexplained knowledge spillover process in the endogenous growth theory may be a crucial factor for a higher level of accuracy in predicting economic growth.

1.2.3 Other Related Growth Theories

The endogenous growth theory and are related to the human capital theory. The endogenous growth theory advocates that improvements in productivity are linked to the growth of the knowledge stock or innovation. Knowledge stock is treated as an endogenous factor of production and a representation of human capital. Formal models of the endogenous growth theory elevate human capital, particularly knowledge, to an increasingly important role in the economics of growth (Romer, 1986; Lucas, 1988; Becker, Murphy and Tamura, 1990; Becker, 1992; Barro and Sala-i-Martin, 1992). The neoclassic growth model only considers the quantity of labor, but quality of labor is not formally modeled as an endogenous growth factor. The interpretation of human capital or knowledge as a factor that drives growth is a progress.

Human capital is typically associated with knowledge and education for most scholars. The seminal work of Schultz (1963) on the human capital theory examined the impact of education investment on agricultural output. The work of Adam Smith, Alfred Marshall, and Milton Friedman, although more sophisticated, did not include education and training investment as factors that drive growth (Becker, 1992). Building on Schultz's theory, Becker (1992) defines

---

[12] The early new growth theory treats knowledge as absolutely non-excludable and thus ignored property rights protection. The later revisions change this knowledge assumption to partially non-excludable or non-rival.

human capital[13] to include knowledge, skills, health, and values, and measures human capital investment through expenditure on formal education, training[14], and medical care. Arrow (1962) interprets human capital as learning-by-doing (Mankiw, 2005). Knowledge and learning include both formal codified knowledge and tacit knowledge (Lundvall and Johnson, 1994; Saxenian, 1994; Foray and Lundvall, 1996).

Newer growth theories posit that the "Solow residual" is even associated with entrepreneurship and innovation (Acs and Evans, 1994; Grossman and Helpman, 1994; Kirzner, 1997; Shane, 2000; Audretsch and Thurik, 2001; Audretsch and Keilbach, 2004). In fact, entrepreneurship is being increasingly recognized as a driver of economic growth. The economic connotation of entrepreneurship originated with Schumpeter (1950), who defined an entrepreneur as a person who is willing and able to convert a new idea or invention into a successful innovation—e.g., new products or new business models. Therefore, entrepreneurship forces "creative destruction" across markets and industries. It is through this "creative destruction" that industries acquire dynamism and contribute to economic growth over the long run. Baumol (2002) has argued that entrepreneurial activity might account for a significant amount of the growth left unexplained in the neoclassic growth models. Entrepreneurial activities contribute to part of the "Solow residual" and explain economic growth because entrepreneurship capital offers a mechanism that facilitates knowledge spillovers from the source creating that knowledge to its commercialization in a third-party (Acs et al., 2004). Entrepreneurs' new ideas and innovation contribute to create new products, services or business models, reduce barriers to knowledge and information spillovers, and thus spur economic growth.

Although empirical testing on this topic has largely developed in the recent years, the link between entrepreneurship capital and economic growth still remains largely anecdotal or based on case studies (Evans and Leighten, 1989). One problem is how to define and measure

---

[13] Becker defined those elements as "human capital" because they are related to human attributes and cannot be separated from individuals' financial and physical assets (Becker 1993). Becker (1992) also suggested that migration, marriage, divorce, family size, and formation of habits could affect human capital.

[14] Particularly on-the-job training.

entrepreneurship capital. The concept of entrepreneurship varies from economic fields to management perspectives. There is no single, consistent definition for entrepreneurship. Audretsch and Keilbach (2004) develop a model of entrepreneurship that incorporates entrepreneurship capital in addition to the neoclassical production function growth model, but this model does not control spatial autocorrelation and agglomeration effects.

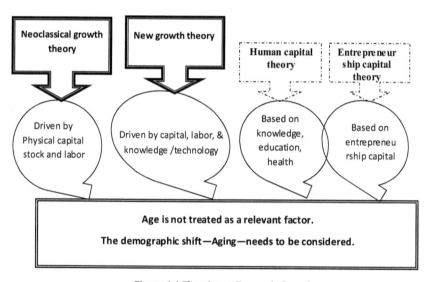

Figure 1.1 Theories on Economic Growth

1.3 Limitations of Current Growth Theories

The progress of the growth theories reflect the economic transformation from the physical capital and labor driven "Fordist Economy" to the knowledge and technology driven "Knowledge Economy". The neoclassical economic theory treats labor, like physical capital, as a factor of production subject to diminishing returns. Although labor efficiency and productivity are considered, it is viewed as being driven by an externally given technology. The endogenous growth theory attempts to interpret the sources of technological change; however, this theory is not yet fully accepted and requires empirical verification. Neither theory considers age as a factor that influences economic growth, nor does the human capital theory or entrepreneurship capital theory. Aging was not a considering context in the growth theory function. Therefore this book particularly addresses the "Knowledge Economy" in the context of aging and argues that aging and the "Knowledge Economy" are two mutually related and beneficial contexts, if public policy directs well.

Chapter 2 Implications of the "Knowledge Economy"--Polycentric Economy & Entrepreneurship

The previous chapter describes what the "Knowledge Economy" is and explains the progress from the "Fordist Economy" to the "Knowledge Economy" from the economic growth theories. As implied in that chapter, the attraction of the "Knowledge Economy" and the reason that the "Knowledge Economy" can progress with incredible economic growth is that this "Knowledge Economy" is driven by new types of capital—knowledge capital (and/or entrepreneurship capital). This new types of capital, differing from the physical capital and labor, can generate non-diminishing returns and has positive externalities. This "Knowledge Economy" relies on information technology and thus become more "footloose". This geographically diffusing situation gradually changes some traditional core-periphery regional economic development structures to polycentric economic development structures. In this specific context, this chapter introduces the polycentric economic structure and its dynamics with entrepreneurship. This polycentric structure offers evidence that the "Knowledge Economy" is less geographically bounded and thus reduces the physical constraints to seniors' labor force participation and occupational choices. This situation makes elderly entrepreneurship more possible.

2.1 Introduction

Classical regional development theories derived from location theory emphasize the core-periphery structure (King, 1985). However, with the development of new information technology and the emerging of the "Knowledge Economy", the traditional core-periphery development pattern in some regions have transformed into a polycentric pattern, such as in Sweden (Johansson, 2002), Central Scotland (Bailey and Turok, 2001), and other European countries (Faludi, 2004). The polycentric regional development pattern has caught increasing attention. Entrepreneurship, which is closely connected with new technology (Autio, 2001) and the "Knowledge Economy" (Atkinson, et al, 1999), may play a critical role in the possible formation and future development of polycentric regional development.

2.2 Core-Periphery Regional Development Framework

Most traditional regional theories assume a core-periphery regional development structure. Considering transportation cost, location theory classifies the areas as core and peripheries within a region. The core, or the central place, is normally an urban area with a larger population and higher density than peripheral areas which are more distant from the center. The core is the center of the regional economy with agglomeration advantages from industry, business, services, technology, education, culture, and policy concentrated there; whereas the peripheries have a more sparse population and are economically less developed. The periphery's development depends on top-down or spillover development effect from the core. This core-periphery structure is particularly reflected in the central place theory.

2.2.1 Central Place Theory

According to King (1985), the two main contributors to central place theory, Walter Christaller (1933) and August Lösch (1940), both describe regional development as core-periphery structure with hierarchies. Christaller (1933) indicates that a larger urban place in the region is normally a higher-order central place and radiates its economy with a larger range of influence or larger tributary and trading areas. The higher-order central place also performs the function of lower-order central place, whereas the lower-order central place is a relative periphery for a higher-order central place; the lowest-order central place, which is a smallest urban area, can only contribute influence to adjacent peripheral areas (Christaller, 1933; Lösch, 1940; Getis and Getis, 1970). Central place theory stresses the development and maintenance of cores through agglomeration effects from various economic activities (King, 1985).

Similar to Christaller (1933) and Lösch (1940)'s central place theory, other location based theories generally classify a region into core and periphery areas with hierarchies. In a big region, the areas outside the highest-order central place or core are peripheries to this core. Thus, the cities smaller than the core are also categorized into peripheral areas relative to the core. In this chapter, a city smaller than the core in a region is called "smaller city". A "smaller city" is a peripheral area to the core.

2.2.2 The Disadvantages of Peripheries and Diseconomies of the Core

Led by this theory and with the effects of economies of scale, many city centers, especially in large cities, have developed into metropolitan centers concentrating industries, business, services, polices, R & D, technology, and human resources (King, 1985). However, with limited spill over effects, the peripheries end up with many disadvantages – increased travel and transport cost resulting from remoteness to the cores, absence of agglomerative advantages, dependence on primary industries, poor local and interregional infrastructure, limited development of R& D and services, and lack of policy influence and initiative (Copus, 2001). Those relative peripheral cities include Manassas, Germantown, Fredericksburg, etc. around Washington D.C. metropolitan area, and Changzhou, Wuhu, Wuxi, etc. around Shanghai metropolitan area in China. Those cities are not very far from the large cities, but with limited spillover effect, their development is limited. Although stage location theories describe this disadvantage of peripheries as temporary and eventually peripheries will develop based on trickling down effects of the core, many peripheries appear to be victims of this "polarization" effect over decades.

33

On the other hand, many core cities become less attractive because of diseconomies of scale, including congestion, limited residential space, old infrastructure, higher taxes and crime (Weida, 2001), eroded environmental quality, and high cost of living. For example, in Washington D.C., the high cost of living, serious congestion, and limited space of housing have made many people choose to live in the suburban areas. The city of Shanghai also has to expand to the original rural suburb because of transportation problems. The old city planning structure can barely accommodate more comfortable housing.

2.3 Entrepreneurship

Although many theorists have explored the notion of entrepreneurship, there exist discrepancies. This section clarifies the concept of entrepreneurship, introduces the key elements supplying entrepreneurship, and explains the entrepreneurial process.

2.3.1 The Concept of Entrepreneurship

Schumpeter (1961), as one of the major theorists for entrepreneurship theories, defines entrepreneurs as the specific persons who

> *"reform or revolutionize the pattern of production by exploiting an invention or, more generally, an untried technological possibility for producing a new commodity or producing an old one in a new way, by opening up a new source of supply of materials or a new outlet for products by reorganizing an industry and so on" (p.132).*

Schumpeter thus emphasizes reforms and revolutionizing the pattern of production as the main quality of entrepreneurs. The reform and revolution is achieved through conduct an untried technological possibility; this reform and revolution can be specified as producing a new

34

commodity, or creating a new way of producing an old commodity, or utilizing a new source of supply, or identifying a new market for products. From Schumpeter's definition, new technological possibility connects entrepreneurship with innovation of a new product or a new industrial structure. Higgins and Savoie (1995) also relate the notion of entrepreneurship to the capacity to introduce new technologies, new products, new resources, and new business organization and management.

Although Schumpeter related entrepreneurship to new technological possibility, entrepreneurship does not only relate to new technology. However, the term "entrepreneurship" in the setting of the "Knowledge Economy" focuses tends to refer to knowledge-based entrepreneurial behavior. Economists have tried various ways to interpret entrepreneurship in terms of its catalyzing role in developing economy. From the macroeconomic level, Cantillon (1755) and Kirzner (1973)'s entrepreneurs establish equilibrium, while Schumpeter (1961)'s entrepreneurs destroy equilibrium and push toward a higher or newer equilibrium position. From microeconomics level, Say (1845) and Marshall (1930) see entrepreneurship as management and decision making process in a firm, while Schumpeter also add innovation into the function. Most economists, except Schumpeter, also emphasize risk bearing as part of entrepreneurship (Van Praag, 1999). Barnett, D. (2000) therefore generalizes entrepreneurship to include the following aspects:

- Innovation by exploring new technological possibility;
- Initiative taking;
- Organizing and reorganizing of social and economic mechanism;
- Risk bearing.

2.3.2 Supply of Entrepreneurship and Entrepreneurial Process

There are basically two forces contributing to the formation of entrepreneurship. One is the individual level and the other is the environment. The individual factors include motivation or need to achieve (McClelland, 1961), willingness to bear risk, desire for independence (Hagen, 1962), and job dissatisfaction (Lordkipanidze, 2002). The environmental forces (or entrepreneurial milieu elements) come from

35

(i)   the private sector, such as capital, professional services, labor market, and business support;

(ii)   social aspects, such as entrepreneurial culture, education, and quality of life;

(iii)   the public sector, such as macro policies, R& D, physical infrastructure, business policies, and public safety, as shown in Figure 2.1 (Rural Development Council, 2001).

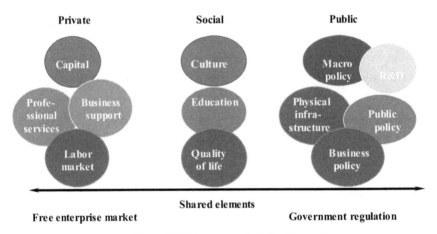

Figure 2.1 Entrepreneurial Milieu Elements
Source: Rural Development Council, 2001.

Environmental and individual forces combine to create entrepreneurship. The entrepreneurial milieu incubates *opportunities* through private and public elements; individual factors explore and exploit the opportunities. Figure 2.2 reviews the formation of entrepreneurship: an opportunity latent environment results in entrepreneurship and may generate a new enterprise when a specific individual recognizes this opportunity as a new value and transfers it into a new economic form (either new product or new business structure).

36

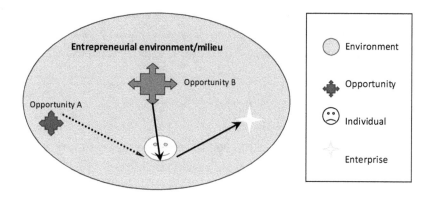

Figure 2.2 Entrepreneurial process

2.4 Entrepreneurial Pattern in Core-Periphery Regional Development Structure

The following sections explore entrepreneurship in regional development patterns-- core-periphery regional develop structure, the "Knowledge Economy", and the polycentric regional development structure. The core-periphery framework is a widely accepted regional development pattern. Many metropolitan areas all over the world fall into this pattern, such as New York, Atlanta, Sidney, Beijing, Shanghai, and Bangkok. It would be interesting to explore whether entrepreneurship in the core-periphery structure pushes a region to grow well and whether it is necessary to develop entrepreneurship in an alternative regional development mode to the core-periphery structure. This section therefore introduces the classic location theory about core-periphery pattern and examines the development of entrepreneurship in this pattern.

When lacking environmental and individual supply for entrepreneurship in the periphery, the core-periphery region becomes an unbalanced entrepreneurial pattern. In the core-periphery structure, productivity factors are highly concentrated in core cities. Many peripheries become subordinate to the core, not just for general economic development, but also for entrepreneurship and knowledge spillover. In the core-periphery structure, as Warntz (1967) stated,

"Space is really the tyranny and distance enforce his rule" (p.7).

Peripheries in this case are only residuals of leftover core activities (Anderson, 2000), including the entrepreneurial activities. As Anderson (2000) described, depending on natural resources driven industries, peripheries basically reproduce the existing pattern of low-order activities and lack higher-order functions. Lower-order natural-resource-dependent economic activities are less able to generate innovation and thus leave little opportunity to add new value. Limited new-value-added innovation opportunities determine that the peripheries are less able to contribute to the entrepreneurial milieu, which results in migration of entrepreneurship into the core (Anderson, 2000). The human resource supply for entrepreneurship is also limited in many peripheries because of the poor knowledge stock or poor knowledge spillover function. Mason also (1991) noted that the awareness of entrepreneurial opportunity depends on the stock of knowledge within the locality.

2.5 Entrepreneurship in the "Knowledge Economy"

Central place theory focusing on the core-periphery regional structure has been influential for decades (King, 1985). In recent years, with the emergence of "footloose" information technology, the core-periphery structure confronts challenge. Many scholars use the term "Knowledge Economy" to address the technological impact on economy. This following section briefly recalls the notion of "Knowledge Economy" that was introduced in Chapter 1 and then examines its relationship with entrepreneurship.

2.5.1 The "Knowledge Economy"

Based on location theory, the core-periphery regional development structure has been a widely accepted model for numerous metropolitan areas all over the world, though in the meantime polarization has brought about various problems for the lagging peripheral areas. In the "Knowledge Economy", economic activities are more technology and knowledge oriented, and service sectors have been taking an increasingly important role in the economy. The "footloose" information technology organizes business structures in a horizontal network that annihilates space differences, and many businesses have successfully outsourced engineering, accounting, marketing, logistics, manufacturing of component parts, etc. (Jarboe and Alliance, 2001). As introduced in the previous chapter, in the "Knowledge Economy", physical location and transportation cost are no longer controlling factors of industry locations, which may shift the location-dominated core-periphery regional economic structure into a new one.

2.5.2 Entrepreneurship in the "Knowledge Economy"

As Chapter 1 illustrates, the growth driver of the "Knowledge Economy" is not capital, labor, or land, but innovation, invention, and knowledge. As implied above, regardless of whether it is the private or public sector, the key element of entrepreneurial milieu lies in innovation opportunities. It is through entrepreneurship that innovation becomes channeled into market value and then pushes the economic growth. One of the few U.S. major entrepreneurship researching organizations, the U.S. National Commission on Entrepreneurship (NCOE), also evidenced the strong association between innovation and entrepreneurship-- since Would War II, entrepreneurs have contributed 67% of innovations and 95% of all radical innovations (NCOE, 2004)[15]. The "Knowledge Economy", driven by innovation that is the first element of the entrepreneurial process, is therefore catalyzed by entrepreneurs. Between 1990-1999 when the "Knowledge Economy" emerged, even in manufacturing industries, entrepreneurial enterprises contributed 45% of total value added by manufacturing (High, 2004). Entrepreneurship is also

---

[15] NCOE and GEM are the major sources for entrepreneurship data. The data showing the relationship between innovation and entrepreneurship might not be the only evidence, but it is the only formal data for this relationship in the author found at the time of writing this paper.

an important part of social capital (Piazza-Georgi, 2002; Higgins and Savoie, 1995) and serves the "Knowledge Economy" through continuous innovation.

2.6 Polycentric Regional Development Framework

The polycentric regional pattern differs in several ways from the core-dominant mononuclear structure, e.g., the core-periphery structure. As shown in Figure 2.3, the mononuclear pattern, such as core-periphery regional development pattern, has a clear dominant core city that has a larger population size and normally develops better than the peripheries with agglomeration effects; in the polycentric pattern, there is no dominant city (or core city) and all cities are similar in size. In the core concentrated regional economy, the peripherals offer various resources to the core city, including natural resources (such as water, energy, iron) and human resources (which is represented by migration from the peripheries into core cities in a region), whereas in the polycentric pattern, all cities have multi-directional mutual cooperative economic relationship.

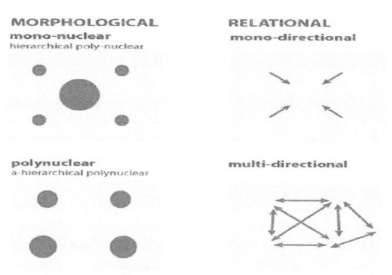

MORPHOLOGICAL
mono-nuclear
hierarchical poly-nuclear

RELATIONAL
mono-directional

polynuclear
a-hierarchical polynuclear

multi-directional

© S. Baudet-Michel, N. Cattan, E. Dumas, UMR Géographie-cités, 2003

Figure 2.3 Contrast Between Mono-nuclear Core-periphery and Polycentric pattern
Source: ESPON, 2003

In the polycentric regional development pattern, the connection between a center and other areas is important. As European Spatial Planning Observation Network (ESPON) (2003) indicates, in the polycentric pattern, distant urban areas, as well as areas with proximity, are connected through two basic types of relation:

(a) institutional co-operation
(b) structural relationships, such as financial flows, telecommunications networks, and exchanges of students.

2.7 Entrepreneurship in the Polycentric Regional Development Structure

The core-periphery pattern highly concentrates entrepreneurship in centers whereas peripheries lack entrepreneurship as a source of innovation and new development. This polarization effect on the one hand results in peripheries lagging economies and on the other hand generates cores' diseconomies of scales. The well-known diseconomies of scales include heavy traffic in commuting, deteriorating natural environment and air quality, and overpriced housing market.

In this situation, it is necessary to examine whether entrepreneurship in the polycentric regional structure can still effectively push economic growth particularly when a metropolis reaches a certain scale. Oriented by information technology and driven by innovation, invention, and knowledge, the "Knowledge Economy" may transfer the core-periphery regional development pattern into a polycentric pattern. Information technology diminishes the traditional role of location and spills over knowledge and information in a location unbounded manner. In the "Knowledge Economy", economic activities and business structure are organized in a horizontal network with little location limitation, as indicated earlier. This horizontal network in the "Knowledge Economy" is a polycentric structure (Copus, 2001). The periphery, the historical victim from core-periphery polarization resulting from locational disadvantage, may no longer be disadvantaged as a remote hinterland in this polycentric economic development model. The peripheral city attached to the core may not be so peripheral; instead, it may become a "center" or "core" itself. As a result, a core-dominated region may be reorganized into regions with multiple centers or multiple "smaller cities"[16] rather than with only a solo "core". Interestingly, this duo- or multi- core concept has already been widely adopted and accepted in the computer field with the current standardized duo-core processor in computer manufacturing.

---

[16] As indicated earlier, a city smaller than the core in a region is called "smaller city" in this paper. A "smaller city" belongs to peripheral areas to the core.

Driven by the "Knowledge Economy" through new technology and innovation, the polycentric regional development model may inevitably have a strong association with entrepreneurship. As indicated earlier, entrepreneurship closely relates to innovation and new technology including information technology, which further determines the close relationship between entrepreneurship and "Knowledge Economy". With the polycentric model as a regional development framework in the "Knowledge Economy", entrepreneurship may thus also have close relationship with polycentric regional pattern.

Considering the fact that entrepreneurship in the core-periphery model might not fully fulfill the potential of every community in a region, exploring the role of entrepreneurship in polycentric economic development model might introduce some new insights. The following section examines the relationship between entrepreneurship and the polycentric model through three perspectives:

(1) whether new technology acts as a media connecting entrepreneurship and polycentric pattern;

(2) whether entrepreneurship pushes the formation of the polycentric structure;

(3) whether the polycentric model pushes entrepreneurship development and thus pushes the development of the whole region.

2.7.1 New Technology Connects Entrepreneurs with the Polycentric Structure

New technology functions as a media between entrepreneurs and polycentric structure because new technology is highly related to both entrepreneurship and the polycentric structure. Firstly, the polycentric structure is new information technology driven. The polycentric pattern is a pattern of regional development in the "Knowledge Economy" and is induced by the effects of rapidly expanding information technology. New technology drives the development of the polycentric structure. As implied above, the "Knowledge Economy" shifts the location dominated mononuclear core-periphery regional structure into a polycentric horizontal network though the "footloose" information technology. Moreover, the polycentric structure uses telecommunication networks to achieve the connectivity for further development (ESPON, 2003).

43

Secondly, technology and entrepreneurship are closely related. On the one hand, new technology brings in innovative opportunities for entrepreneurial behavior. As Shumpeter (1961) indicated, entrepreneurs use new technological possibilities to realize innovation of a new product or a new business organization. In the "Knowledge Economy", new technology includes new information technology or Information Communication Technology (ICT), which increased the availability of exploitable information (Audretsch, 2001). Without the ICT "revolution", the imperfect market with information asymmetry makes entrepreneurial firms particularly susceptible (Felsenstein and Fleischer, 2002). Better information flow that is brought about by the ICT "revolution" makes markets more transparent and innovative opportunities become more visible.

On the other hand, the new technology further expands entrepreneurial capacity. The new technology results in the diffusion of technological and scientific knowledge. The diffusion of technology and knowledge makes it easier for people to diversify skills and to learn about entrepreneurial methods (Suarez-Villa, 2004), and to recognize where the innovative opportunities are, which in turn catalyzes entrepreneurial behavior. Finally, entrepreneurship can push the development of new technology by innovative use of current technology and invention of new technology. Figure 2.4 reviews the above discussion and visualizes that close relationship and mutually catalyzing roles between entrepreneurship and new technology; together they serve to develop the polycentric regional economic model.

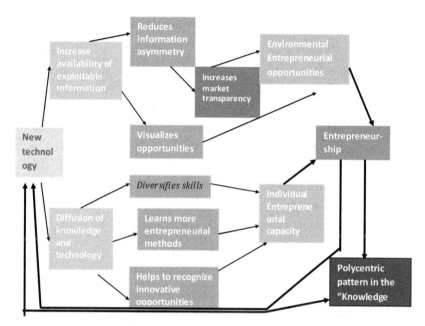

Figure 2.4 Dynamic Relationship between New technology, Entrepreneurship, and Polycentric Economic Development Pattern

The Global Entrepreneurship Monitor (GEM) Report evidenced the close relationship between entrepreneurship and new technology. According to GEM dataset in July 2000, the correlation between Internet hosts per 10,000 people and firm-Sponsored start-ups is as high as 0.56, and this correlation is statistically significant at the 0.001 level; the correlation between Internet hosts per 10, 000 people and entrepreneurial opportunity is 0.53, and this correlation is statistically significant at the 0.01 level (Autio, 2001). As entrepreneurship and new technology are highly correlated and as the polycentric model is new technology driven, new technology thus connects entrepreneurship and the polycentric structure.

2.7.2 Entrepreneurs Help to Shape the Polycentric Regional Development Framework

The entrepreneurship theories suggest that, without entrepreneurship to initiate or drive development of peripheral cities, new technology cannot automatically transfer core-periphery regional structure into a polycentric pattern, even though new technology may directly contribute to the polycentric urban economic pattern. As indicated earlier, the development on the peripheries has lagged with its poorly developed infrastructure and low-order industrial activities. In the opinion of the author, to eliminate these disadvantages and to develop the periphery requires innovations and investment to bring in new market values. However, there is high uncertainty and risk in sufficiently investing into the peripheries to turn it into "centers". Therefore, this situation requires people who

(1) are motivated to explore the new value added opportunities,

(2) have the vision and skills to exploit new technological possibilities and to bring in new value through innovation,

(3) are able to take initiative,

(4) are willing to bear risks.

Those requirements match exactly the definition of entrepreneurs. Figure 2.5 reviews the above discussion about the match between requirements to develop a center and qualities of entrepreneurs, as analyzed above. Thus, entrepreneurs are needed to develop the periphery into a new center and to contribute to the evolution to the polycentric structure.

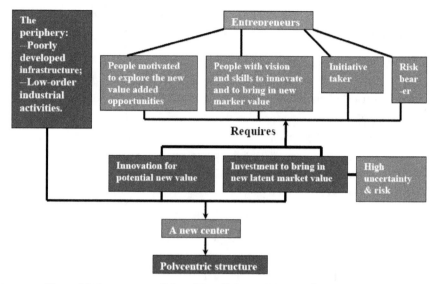

Figure 2.5 Entrepreneurs Help to Shape Polycentric Regional Structure

After the new center emerges, to sustain its growth as a center, continued innovation with new market values is needed. At this moment, entrepreneurship is also critical because entrepreneurship either directly innovates or transfers innovative concepts into market values after taking initiatives, bearing risks, and making decisions with vision and skills. Thus, entrepreneurship, as a basic format of social capital (Higgins and Savoie, 1995; Piazza-Georgi, 2002), would be a key element to push the new center's development and to reinforce the polycentric regional economic structure.

2.7.3 Polycentric Entrepreneurship Network—"Smaller Cities" Turn into New Entrepreneurial Hubs

Peripheries under the core-periphery regions include "smaller cities" and rural areas. "Smaller cities" are peripheral centers, including edge cities defined by Garreau (1991) and other suburban cities and urban villages. Garreau (1991) uses Tysons Corner, Virginia as an example to describe "smaller city" at major suburban freeway interchanges as the latest transformation of people's life and work. Lang (2003) lists many emerging edge cities locating around major core cities and developing fast in recent years. Those emerging edge cities include Costa Mesa around Los Angeles, Post Oak around Houston, Cumberland Galleria around Atlanta, Southfield around Detroit, and LBJ Freeway around Dallas.

"Smaller cities" develop well because they have special advantage over both core cities and rural areas and accommodate business needs better than either core cities or rural locations. "Smaller cities" are superior to dispersed rural locations due to their industrial and information infrastructure and certain level of agglomeration of economic activities; compared with core cities, "smaller cities" do not have the long list of negative externalities resulting in diseconomies of scales and out-migration. "Smaller cities" have good business environments and can attract more human resources, which in turn contributes to generating an entrepreneurial milieu[17] with innovative opportunities.

In the opinion of the author, once a "smaller city" emerges with business infrastructure and networks that are mature enough to become a new center, this new center will attract more resources (including material and social capital) and agglomerate its various economic resources into a better and better entrepreneurial milieu. The good entrepreneurial milieu becomes a new entrepreneurial hub. Thus, "smaller cities" function as new entrepreneurial hubs and emerge as new centers. If many new centers emerge in one region and the polycentric structure becomes well defined, the polycentric region simultaneously becomes a polycentric entrepreneurship network, with the new centers as entrepreneurship hubs.

---

[17] As explained earlier, an entrepreneurial milieu is an entrepreneurial environment.

48

As Suarez-Villa (2004) states, nodes or hubs often articulate the spatial dimensions of networks, and nodes are sources of change and innovation for the surrounding areas in the network. This function of nodes or hubs suggests when "smaller cities" emerge into new centers and new entrepreneurial nodes emerge, entrepreneurship can further diffuse to surrounding rural areas. Although rural areas may find it more difficult to become entrepreneurial hubs due to lack of agglomeration of economic activities, the polycentric regional development framework can still contribute to the transfer of some entrepreneurial opportunities to these areas. With nearby "smaller cities" as new entrepreneurial hubs, more entrepreneurs may reconsider the heavily natural resources dependent rural areas as locations for their ventures, for example, exploring new values from tourism in rural areas.

Figure 2.6 reviews the whole process of developing a new center initiated with exploiting new technological possibilities that require entrepreneurship supplied both endogenously in the new center and exogenously from a core city. Although new technology is not the only drive for a city to develop, in the setting of the "Knowledge Economy", the role of new technology becomes eminent.

To initiate new development through technology in the "Knowledge Economy", entrepreneurs investing in technological infrastructure are needed. However, in core-periphery regional pattern, lacking agglomeration effect and sustainable industry structure, local entrepreneurial elements in peripheries flow into the core cities. Thus, to initiate building the technological infrastructure, exogenous entrepreneurs attracted to peripheries would be very helpful. Once the new technology is introduced and used after new infrastructure is built, the new technology directly supplies information, spillover knowledge and skills, and motivates more entrepreneurship. This would further spur creativity, innovation and invention. At this stage, innovative people with visions and skills who are also willing to bear risk become entrepreneurs and add new values to the market though innovating a new product or a new organization. The new values eventually contribute to economic development of this center and help to reinforce it as a new economic center and potential entrepreneurship hub. The new center with a growing population of entrepreneurs will then explore and exploit new values though technology again. The entrepreneurship and development cycle progresses. Consequently, this area becomes an entrepreneurship driven new center and a new entrepreneurial hub of the whole region.

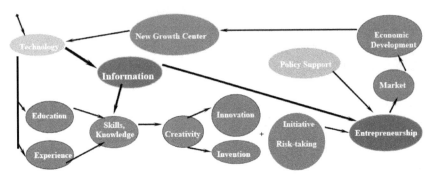

Figure 2.6 Entrepreneurship and Developing New Growth Center[18]

2.8 Conclusion: Policy Implications for Entrepreneurship in Polycentric Economic Structure

This chapter explores a new entrepreneurship related regional economic model in the "Knowledge Economy"—polycentric economic development model. Entrepreneurship in the core-periphery regional development model is concentrated in the core, while the peripheries lack entrepreneurship. In the "Knowledge Economy", entrepreneurship becomes a catalyst for economic growth and the polycentric regional development structure becomes a new regional development model. Entrepreneurship and polycentric regional pattern has close relationship--

---

[18] Although new technology here is graphed as the initial drive of the new center 's formation, it does not negate the role of other economic elements, such as population, economic infrastructures, and institutional framework. This paper emphasizes the role of new technology, so technology is shown here as the initial drive, by no means the only initial drive.

new technology connects entrepreneurs with the polycentric structure, entrepreneurs help to shape the polycentric regional development framework, and polycentric structure is also a polycentric entrepreneurship network with "smaller cities" as new entrepreneurial hubs.

The exploration of the theoretical possibility for the polycentric structure shows that polycentric structure is the regional development model spurred by the information technology in the "Knowledge Economy", and this model is more sustainable than the traditional core-periphery model. This new model not only grants developing opportunities to peripheries, but also helps to mitigate the core's negative externalities and diseconomies of scale. Eventually the advantage of the polycentric structure is to achieve a large potential of a region with more balanced opportunity redistribution.

To push or motivate formation of the information-technology driven polycentric pattern, it would be helpful to build information infrastructure necessary to their economic development in the "smaller cities" because information infrastructure provides the basic hardware for better entrepreneurial information flow and prevents technological divide in the economies between core cities and peripheries. Building information infrastructure needs to be combined with development of economic base and a certain population base that brings in capital flow and innovation. Just developing infrastructure without the development of other related economic components would be a waste of resources. Moreover, new technology is a double-edged sward. New technology is not costless and equally efficiently implementable everywhere based on different economic structure and background in cities. Thus, building information infrastructure maximizing its cost-benefit effect for economic development is an important start for "smaller cities" emergence into new centers and entrepreneurial hubs.

To build the "smaller cities" into new centers, promoting some special policies to offer more entrepreneurial opportunities would be necessary. As building information infrastructure is expensive and risking, attracting entrepreneurs as risk bearers and initiative takers to identify the new value of the peripheries and channel latent value into business markets is extremely important. To attract entrepreneurs, providing the entrepreneurial opportunities is the key to forming an entrepreneurial milieu. This situation requires good macro policies.

Further, to create a good entrepreneurial milieu in the new centers, special policies to promote entrepreneurial opportunities include policies to attract outside entrepreneurs and to motivate "endogenous" entrepreneurs, such as providing better housing options and quality of life, implementing fiscal and monetary policies to support higher potential profits, and developing R & D funding to enhance the asset base for entrepreneurial ventures. Compared to core cities' diseconomies of scale, the better housing options and better quality of life in the new centers would be attractive to entrepreneurs who are not satisfied with crowded life with limited quality in core cities. Better fiscal and monetary policy can motivate entrepreneurs to invest for more profits. Developing R & D funding offers the source of the enhancement of entrepreneurial milieu and can motivate more entrepreneurship development in the long run.

Lastly, once the new centers that are simultaneously entrepreneurial hubs emerge in the peripheral area surrounding a core city, another important strategy for polycentric regional development pattern is to develop the education system to supply sustainable endogenous entrepreneurship. Education system related to entrepreneurship growth includes schools, colleges, media, and community libraries. A good education system improves the awareness of entrepreneurial opportunity and enhances knowledge and skill base in the labor pool.

This study analyzes entrepreneurship in two different regional development structures based on general theoretical reasoning. Future research focusing on case studies and empirical data to prove this theoretical research would be helpful. For example, it is not known yet whether the above theoretical argument is consistent with the empirical data. Equally important is to clarify a commonly acceptable measurement of entrepreneurship.

Part III Aging

Chapter 3 Aging, a Long-Term Demographic Trend[19]

The previous part interprets what the "Knowledge Economy" is. Chapter 1 described the characteristics in the "Knowledge Economy" and Chapter 2 observed the regional development model change from the traditional location-bounded core-periphery structure to the polycentric structure. Different from the previous economies, the "Knowledge Economy" not only has new economic growth drivers as knowledge, innovation, entrepreneurship, and technology, but is also fundamentally changing the whole economic framework. Physical labor and location seem less important than before. Yet, this economic progress is not the only unique historical background that we are facing. This major economic shift coincidentally intersects with a fundamental demographic change—aging. This part, Part III of this book, addresses the aging trend in the U.S. population.

The U.S. population is aging and seniors continue to comprise a larger proportion of the population. As a result of a declining mortality rate and staying low fertility rate, the U.S. population is aging. There are two major forces result in the demographic aging trend—one is the reduced mortality rate and lengthened life span, and the other is the declining fertility rate. The reduced mortality rate and lengthened life span result from continuously enhancing medical, health, and living conditions. As illustrated in Figure 3.1, the U.S. average life expectancy at birth in 1900 was only 47 years, but in 2000 is 76.9 years; for a baby born in 2050, this figure is projected to reach 82.6 (U.S. Census Bureau, 2001).

---

[19] Part of the literature review in this chapter is excerpted from Zhang (2008).

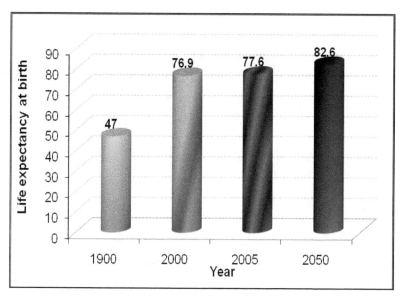

Figure 3.1 Life Expectancy at Birth Comparison in the United States, 1900-2050
Data Source: U.S. census Bureau. (2001); CIA World Factbook (2005).

At the same when mortality rate is decreasing and life span is lengthened, fertility rates of the U.S. population stay no higher than the replacement rate that is 2.11 births per women. In 2000, the U.S. total fertility rate is 2.056; in 2001, this figure shrinks to 2.034 (Haub, 2003; Population Research Bureau, n.d.); in 2005, this figure is estimated at 2.08 (CIA World Factbook, 2005). Consequently, seniors aged 65 or over take a growing proportion among total U.S. population. As shown in Figure 3.2, seniors aged 65 or above in 1900 only accounted for approximately 4% of the U.S. population; Now, the size of the 65+ cohort has grown to 35 million and accounts for 12.4 % of the U.S. population (U.S. Administration on Aging, 2002; CIA World Factbook, 2005).

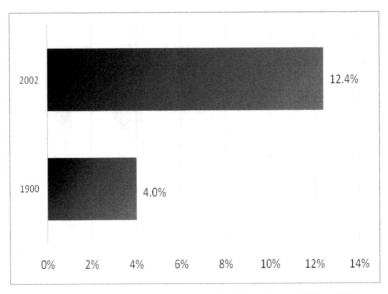

Figure 3.2 Proportions of Older People in Total U.S. Population, 1900 vs. 2002
Data Source: U.S. Administration on Aging, 2002

3.1 Baby Boomers

The baby boomer generation (i.e., those who were born from year 1946 to year 1964) expedites the aging process in the next decades. This baby boomer generation has created population driven dynamics in U.S. society at each of its development stage: from the moment when baby boomers were teens to their adulthood and to their current senior ages. This generation has affected U.S. society from every aspect, such as education, employment, and consumption. When this generation was at school ages, education resource was a major socioeconomic issue; when this generation reached employment ages, policies were created to settle their jobs; now when this generation approaches retirement ages, Social Security, Medicare, and many other aging-related issues become prominent social concerns.

Baby boomers' role in the U.S. population can also be seen in the age pyramid. Age pyramid of the U.S. population illustrates the aging process and trend through an increasingly large proportion of older persons in the total population. Appendix 3.1 contrasts the age pyramids of the United States in the year 1975 and 2000 and projected population pyramid of 2025 and 2050. In these pyramids, each horizontal bar represents a 5-year birth cohort. The younger birth cohorts are located at the bottom of the pyramids and the top ones represent the older birth cohorts. In the year-1975 age pyramid, the bottom bulge for ages 10-29 represents the baby boomer generation. In the year-2000 age pyramid, the middle bulge represents the baby boomer generation and the bottom bulge represents the echo boomer generation. The Echo boomer generation is composed of the offspring of baby boomers and therefore is called "echo" of the baby boomer generation. In the year-2025 age pyramid, the top bulge is for baby boomers and the middle bulge is for echo boomers. However, the bulges in the year-2025 age pyramid are not as evident as the year-1975 and year-2000 age pyramids. In 2050, there seem no bulges any further; instead, the age pyramid is transformed into a rectangular shape.

The population pyramids, from the census population estimation in 1975 to its population projection in 2050, show a ballooning top: during the period of 1975-2050, the shape of the population pyramid changes from approximately triangle-like pyramid in 1975 to a rectangular cylindrical form in 2050, with even a ballooning top for ages over 85. The shift from a triangle shape to a rectangular shape pyramid indicates that the U.S. population is aging and older people take a bigger and bigger proportion among total population. This ballooning top in the 2050 population pyramid is especially prominent for women aged 85 and above.

3.2 The "Demographic Transition Model"

Although baby boomers that are entering retirement age are normally considered a source for the population to age, they are not the only source for the aging population. Instead, the trend of aging is projected to be inevitable. In Warren Thompson's "Demographic Transition Model", aging is the fourth stage of demographic transition process.

The "Demographic Transition Model" is an idealized model that describes population changes over time, based on the historical experience of Western European developed countries.

In this model, the demographic transition process is presented through the relationships between the birth rate (e.g. Crude Birth Rate or CBR), the death rate (e.g. Crude Death Rate or CDR), and the population growth (Weeks, 2005). The whole population growth experience is divided into four stages:

I.   Pre-industrial,

II.   Transitional,

III.   Industrial, and

IV.   Postindustrial stage.

As shown in Figure 3.3, Stage I shows a low-growth balance, called the "primitive stability", between a high birth rate and a high death rate. Then, the improved food, nutrition, health and medical conditions resulted in a "mortality transition". With this "mortality transition", Stage II is comprised of a high birth rate, a low death rate, and thus a high population growth rate. The high population growth occurs with migration and urbanization. In Stage III, due to feminism movement and cultural changes, the birth rate, called the "fertility transition", starts to decline as well as the death rate.

Starting from the "mortality transition" in Stage II, people's life span become longer, and the total population becomes older. The "fertility transition" that occurred since Stage III accelerates the population to become even older; in Stage IV, with a low fertility rate and a low mortality rate, the population is stably aging. This stability is called "modern stability" to contrast to the "primitive stability" in Stage I. According to this "Demographic Transition Model, both of the decreased mortality rate and the decreased fertility rate directly contribute to population aging.

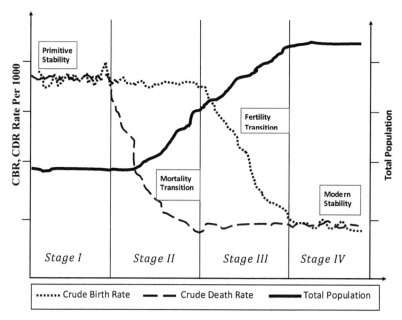

Figure 3.3 the Demographic Transition Model
Note: This figure is drawn based on Warren Thompson's Concept of Demographic Transition
Model in Weeks (2005).

3.3 The Demographic Transition Process in the United States

The experiences of the current developed countries, including the United States, are similar to the above demographic transition model and most of them are now in stage IV. Shown in Figure 3.4, the U.S. population entered Stage IV roughly in the 1990s and this status of the "modern stability", or Stage IV, with aging seems to persist for many more years. Since Americans are living longer and the fertility rate still stays below the replacement rate, the U.S. population will continue the trend of aging. The decreased mortality rate and the low-than-replacement-rate fertility rate directly result in population aging. This aging trend is, thus, not necessarily due to baby boomers.

The major wave of the Crude Birth Rate (CBR) curve in Figure 3.4 indicates the baby boomers. The smaller wave of the CBR curve indicates the echo boomers that reflects the next generation of baby boomers and thus echoes the birth cohort wave of the baby boomer generation. Although the wave representing the baby boomers is evident, it is not the only force that determines the general aging trend. As shown in the U.S. population transition process (Figure 3.4), baby boomers only compose a small part of the later stages in the U.S. demographic transition chart. Although the aging of baby boomers expedites the U.S. population aging process, it is not the beginning, main stream, or the ending of the population aging, according to the current demographic trends. The general aging trend seems inevitable, even without baby boomers. This aging trend will not disappear with the disappearance of baby boomers.

Although the demographic transition model did not consider cross-country migration and although immigrants in the United States contribute to the U.S. population and economic growth, international immigrants still stay a relatively low proportion among the total U.S. population. The limited quantity of immigrants, relative to the total population size, has a limited impact on the general trend of the overall U.S. population.

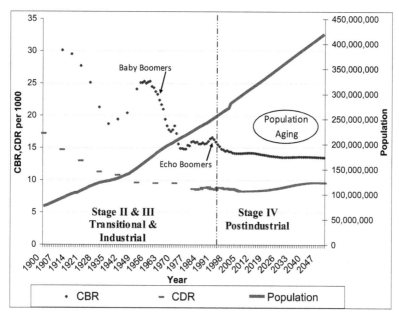

Figure 3.4 Demographic Transition Model in the United States
Data Source: U.S. Census Bureau.

Since the aging trend will possibly not disappear with the exit of baby boomers from the population, mitigating the aging related crises will not be meaningful just for the next decade or two. Concentrating on the issues resulted from an aging population will relate to the long-run future of the U.S. economy and society.

Chapter 4 Aging: Work Force Shortage and Fiscal Crisis[20]

What could population aging imply? As a long-term demographic trend, the aging implications would be of a long term as well, if no further policy practice were taken. Aging, as being perceived to be a non-welcoming term, has been projected to result in challenging crises in the next decades to come, particularly for labor and finance. This chapter documents the predicted aging resulted labor shortage and fiscal crisis.

4.1 Aging Resulted Labor Shortage

U.S. labor force is aging with the U.S. population, the. Younger workers comprise a declining proportion of total employment, along with the shrinking cohorts for younger people. According to data from the U.S. Bureau of Labor Statistics, Figure 4.1 exhibits the dramatic change in the age structure of the labor force. From 1994 to 2002, employment growth rate for younger people (aged 25-54 in this figure) shows a slowdown and eventual declines following 2000. As a contrast, employment growth rate for people aged 55 and over (this includes the leading edge of baby boomers) is rising increasingly fast. With more and more baby boomers reaching retirement ages, the U.S. labor force is expected to age even more in the next two decades.

---

[20] Part of the literature review in this chapter is excerpted from Zhang (2008).

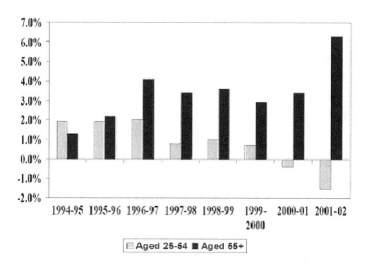

Figure 4.1 Percent Change in the Number of Employed Persons Aged 25-54 and 55+, 1994-2002
Source: U.S. Department of Labor, Bureau of Labor Statistics January 1995-January 2003.

In addition to the aging population, there is an additional factor driving U.S. labor force to age. While the U.S. labor force has continued to age, *the average retirement age* has actually *declined* since 1950 (Social Security Administration, 1999). Between 1970 and 2000, the average retirement age decreased from 66.2 (Ippolito, 1990) to 62 (Gendell, 2001). Ippolito (1990) indicated that the average retirement age from full-time and part-time work declined from 66.2 in 1970 to 64.1 in 1985. In 1995, the average retirement age for American men is 63.6 and for women is 61.6 (Blöndal and Scarpetta, 1999). Although Johnson (2001) critiqued on Blöndal and Scarpetta (1999)'s measurement of average retirement age, the average retirement age estimated by the Bureau of Labor Statistics (BLS) and Social Security Administration is basically consistent with what Blöndal and Scarpetta (1999) has indicated: the average retirement age for the period of 1995-2000 is about 62.0 for men and 61.4 for women, though the estimation from Social Security series is normally slightly higher than the labor force series (Gendell 2001).

63

With current policies and various historical incentives for early retirement, many workers aged 55 or over will possibly withdraw from the labor force soon. With the withdrawal of baby boomers from the labor force and also with insufficient supplements to the labor force from the younger cohorts, the U.S. labor force will continue to shrink. If there are no major technological innovations that largely reduce requirements for labor, a short-run labor force shortage could consequently result, as Peterson (1999) and Schetagne (2001) suggested.

Several policy options have been proposed to mitigate the labor force shortage, but they all have limitations. For example, although this labor force shortage has been in part and will likely in part be offset by immigrants, politically the United States cannot admit too many immigrants and cannot totally rely on immigrants to solve the labor shortage problem. The later section (Section 4.3) in this chapter summarizes the policy options that are proposed to mitigate the labor shortage and evaluates their limitations in details.

As a result, the elderly dependency ratio (defined by age in this figure) is increasing, as shown in Figure 4.2. By 2050, the total dependency ratio is projected to surpass 65%, and this increasingly high dependency ratio is largely the result of the enlarging retirement population. In another word, it is the Elderly Dependency Ratio (EDR), instead of Younger Dependency Ratio (YDR), that leads to the increase in the overall dependency ratio. Starting from year 2030, a working-age person will need to support himself/herself, at least a 1/3 of an elderly person who is aged 65 and above, and a 1/3 of a child. What is behind the increasing dependency ratio is not just the looming labor shortage, but also the fiscal crises.

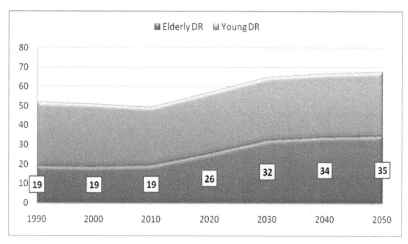

Figure 4.2 Dependency Ratio (DR) in the United States, 1990-2050
Data source: U.S. Census Bureau.

It should be noted though that the dependency ratio does not accurately reflect the ratio of non-working people to working people. This is because age is not necessarily the determinant of a person's participation in the labor force. In this case, the age-defined dependency ratio is used only as a proxy to the ratio of non-working people to working people.

4.2 Fiscal Crisis

In the meantime when the looming labor shortage crisis approaches, a financial crisis would result from the aging population as well. With the increasingly large retirement cohort and under current policy and technology conditions, a financial crisis of social services is imminent. The declining retirement age, compared to decades ago, and thus longer life after retirement would further deepen this labor shortage. Social Security, Medicare, and national health expenditures on the senior population comprise an increasingly large percentage of the federal budget. Figure 4.3 illustrates this situation. In 1970, Social Security represented 15.5% of federal budget and Medicare about 3.2%; in 2001, these percentages had increased to 23% and 12%, respectively, according to Hooymann and Kiyak (2005).

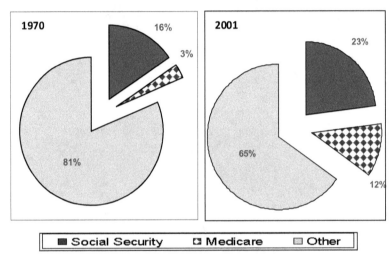

Figure 4.3 Federal Budget Allocation I 1970 versus 2001
Note: This figure is drawn based on Hooymann and Kiyak (2005).

Americans aged 65 or over consume 36% of national health expenditures, which is four times higher than that for younger cohorts (with ages less than 65) (Callaban, 2000). The U.S. Census projected that the number of Americans aged 62 and over will double in the next three decades and all will be eligible to claim Social Security benefits. This will mean seniors will consume at least eight times higher national health expenditures than younger cohorts in the next three decades, assuming the size of younger cohorts stays the same. This will surely add much more pressure to government expenditure. In this background, the eligible age for full Social Security benefits is legislated to increase eventually to 67 to reduce the fiscal pressure (Social Security Advisory Board, 1999; Bruce, et al., 2000). Duval (2003) notes that early labor market

66

withdrawal comes at the expense of living standards of the later generations because retirement benefits are financed through payroll taxes. Greenspan (2004) thus emphasized the need for the government to recalibrate public programs, or the economy will not be able to deliver sufficient benefits to retirees.

Social Security income is an important source of income for seniors. The initial Social Security Act (Act of August 14, 1935) paid retirement benefits only to the primary workers and Social Security benefits was not meant to support all needs of individuals in the old age but rather as a supplemental resource; however, the Social Security benefits have been expanded over the past decades and nowadays comprise an important part of income to many seniors. According to Social Security Administration (2004), Social Security benefits comprised 39 percent of the aggregate income of the aged population (of age 65 and over) in 2003; Social Security was the only source of income for 21 percent of American seniors in 2003, and it comprises over 90 percent of the total income for 34 percent of American seniors in 2003.

Without improved policies, the financial crisis in the coming decades will be worse. Bruce, et al. (2000) indicates that under the current policies and the Social Security Trustees' intermediate assumptions, annual expenditures on the Old age, Survivors and Disability programs (OASDI) is expected by the year 2016 to exceed the OASDI tax income that comes from the payroll. This will also exceed all sources of income. These sources of income include the taxes and interest earned on Trust Fund reserves that are expected to come in by 2025. The Board of Trustees (2000) indicates that by 2037, the accumulated OASDI trust funds could be exhausted, and anticipated receipts would be able to cover only about 70% of anticipated expenditures.

4.3 Solutions to the Labor force Shortage and Fiscal Pressure

To avoid the potential labor and fiscal crisis, some are considering various policy options. These include cutting back benefits, raising taxes, and taking measures to enlarge the labor force (see Peterson, 1999; Herman et al., 2003). As Zhang (2008) explained in details, many of the above approaches could help to reduce the labor force shortage; however, they all have certain limitations. In the meantime, retiring later and working longer might help to fundamentally mitigate the labor force shortage in a big magnitude. The aged cohort is growing. Working longer while seniors are still interested in working could help to reduce the number of senior dependents, improve the elderly dependency ratios and consequently, contribute to the Social Security fund contribution. This strategy could even improve seniors' satisfaction of life for those who would like to continue fulfilling their career enjoyment (Hooymann and Kiyak 2005). According to the age pyramids in Appendix 3.1, seniors will take an increasingly large proportion among total population. Plus, encouraging a longer working life will not exclude other approaches to mitigate the aging-related crises. These older people include women and immigrants. If everyone could work a bit longer with their accumulated working experience and skills, the elderly "dependents" could turn into elderly "supporters". Since people are living longer, healthier, and better educated than before, physically people have a better capacity to work longer. With healthier conditions, working could also help to reduce boredom. Continuing working is in this sense consistent with the concept of "successful aging" that implies that keeping active and productive in late life can increase older people's life satisfaction (Hooymann and Kiyak, 2005).

Many scholars purported the idea of retiring later. Bruce, et al. (2000) predict that future generations of workers could decide to remain in the labor force longer than current workers, and that these workers will rely more on earnings rather than Social Security funds for their economic well-being in the later stages of life. Based on theoretical and empirical analysis, Duval (2003) also offers a similar insight and suggests that seniors' participation in the labor force can ease the adjustment to aging population by curbing the age-related expenditure increase. Actually, the enlarged labor force participation through increased seniors' involvement can result in higher tax revenue and thus generate broader revenue for an enhanced welfare system to seniors as a whole, which provides a more solid financial basis for senior' late life satisfaction.

However, even if the policy orients to encourage seniors' later retirement, there mifght exist a certain quantity of seniors who would not like to return to the labor force or resist retiring later. The next two sections thus focus on exploring the disincentives and incentives for a later retirement.

4.4 Disincentives for Later Retirement

The issue of retiring later in life is a controversial concern for both employers and seniors themselves. In the private sector, many employer pension plans penalize older workers through benefit calculation rules that reduce the value of expected pension benefits for additional years of work on that job (Bruce, et al., 2000). This situation might, though, gradually change. Many employers are still concerned about the higher cost[21] and lower productivity generated by older people[22] (Crown and Longino, 2000). For many people, older people are perceived as being technically obsolete. More over, there are many other personal and social factors that discourage an older person to continue working beyond retirement. Some of these factors include increased income (Clark et al., 1999), their own failing health or their family members' failing health, financial incentives for early retirement (Ippolito, 1990; Committee for Economic Development, 1999; Crown and Longino, 2000; Remery, et al., 2003), job loss, difficult bosses or coworkers, age discrimination (Rix, 2004), etc.

4.4.1 Historical Early Retirement Incentives

As indicated earlier, there has been a trend of early retirement since the 1950s. Various factors contributes to this declining retirement age. From the labor supply side, personal decision of retirement is an issue of individual choice, which has certain level of heterogeneity and is, to a large extent, a product of social-economic culture. From the labor demand side, the incentives for early retirement include policy incentives for early retirement in some companies, new technology requirement, and stereotypes against seniors. Crown and Longino (2000) also indicate that some policies encourage early retirement, such as financial incentives for Social

---

[21] Higher labor cost is because of higher level of absenteeism, higher health insurance cost, pensions, higher income level matching with their longer working experiences (Thurow, 1975; Lazear, 1998), and some government regulation of employee benefits.

[22] Perceived lower productivity is associated with their obsolete skills (Crown and Longino, 2000) and stereotype against them, such as ailing, less efficient, with slow reaction, limited learning capacity, etc (AARP, n.d.; Barth et al., 1993; Guillemar et al., 1996; Henkens, 2000; Sokolovsky, 2000; Taylor & Walker, 1998; Wagner, 1998).

Security and private pension plans. The following subsections explain those incentives in details.

4.4.2 Individuals' Retirement Decisions

Although retirement is basically a voluntary decision in the United States, there are many personal factors influencing seniors' decision for the timing of retirement. Clark et al (1999) compared data across states in the United States and found that increases in income per capita over long periods played a significant role in the decline in older men's labor force participation. With the income increase, many young older people (aged 65-74) choose to retire for leisure that is prevented by their working schedules. However, leisure or travel is not the only attraction for Americans to retire. Many of them retire because of needs to take care of their beloved ones, or because of their own failing health, or because of the unpleasant working experience and working environment. Research from American Association of Retired Persons (AARP) Public Policy Institute has found that job loss, health problems, and care giving responsibilities are among the incentives to appeal retirement as well as difficult bosses or coworker and age discrimination (Rix, 2004).

4.4.3 Financial Incentive for Retirement

Public policy usually plays an important role in intervening market behavior, particularly when the policy can be used for profitability. The early retirement incentive programs (ERIPS) in the late 1970s and early 1980s have been very effective and its influence can still persist now. ERIPS was developed to vacate more working opportunities for the large young baby boomer cohort and thus gave older people more time to enjoy the rest of their life. However, it has been used as an excuse for employers to reduce their older personnel for cost consideration without exposing themselves to charges of age discrimination (Crown and Longino, 2000). Now facing the workforce shortage, public policy tend to orient later retirement, but ERIPS would still take time to exit the market. Although several policies that include 1978 Amendments to the Age Discrimination in Employment Act, 1983 Social Security amendments, and Social Security Retirement Trust Fund contained provisions designed to encourage later retirement, those

70

policies are only partially effective and receive smaller than anticipated effects (Crown and Longino, 2000).

Among various public policies, financial policies often have the strongest impact. Private pension plans and Social Security discourage older people to continue working because they penalize work after some age (Committee for Economic Development, 1999), often as low as age 55. Working after this age will reduce the value of lifetime pension benefits and thus creates an implicit "tax". Remery et al (2003), based on Dutch experience, directly pointed out that older workers tended to be in a particularly vulnerable position during economic recession because early retirement was often seen as a less painful approach to reduce the labor supply than large-scale layoffs. The U.S. economic sluggish in the late 1980s and early 1990s compounded with early retirement wave has downsized the age of the U.S. labor force and many older workers have exited from the labor force. In 1950, the labor force participation rate of older people aged 65 or over was 42%; in 1970 this figure declined to 27%; by 1985, this labor force participation rate for older people dropped to only 16% (Ippolito, 1990). Although recent labor force participation rate of older people began to slightly rebound due to various reasons (see Appendix 4.1), according to data from Bureau of Labor Statistics, early retirement trend still has its momentum so that the actual retirement age in 2000 has not yet increased much from the age of 62.

4.4.4 Structural and Cultural Disincentive for Employment

In addition to older people's voluntary decisions of withdrawing the labor force, there are also structural and cultural disincentives for them to continue working. Seniors tend not to be the vanguards of technology innovation. Older people are more vulnerable to skill obsolescence, which shrinks their value to employers. Many employers concern about the higher costs and lower productivity generated by the older employees, relative to the younger ones (Crown and Longino, 2000). Productivity, to a large extent, depends on workers' skill levels. Older people's obsolete skills devalue their productivity or profitability toward employers, which thus composes a big concern of hiring older people. Employing older people is normally associated with higher labor cost because of higher income matching with their longer working experiences, higher level of absenteeism, higher health insurance cost, some government regulation of employee benefits, and pensions.

Many seniors also lack job hunting skills or do not keep up with the skills needed for the current job market. For those seniors who retired for a while and who had been working for an employer for a long time and did not change jobs as often as the younger ones, lacking job hunting techniques is one structural disincentive for older people to continue working (Hooyman & Kiyak, 2005).

Older ages, particularly working in the similar track of position for a long time, are often associated with higher income. Thurow (1975) introduces a "Seniority Principle". This principle suggests that income and productivity are not always related across a worker's career. During the first phase of workers' career while they are younger, their earnings are lower than their productivity; during the second phase with older ages, their earnings are higher than their productivity (Lazear, 1998). During the older ages, when productivity begins to decline, their earnings do not necessarily decline; but the "overpaid" earnings are normally a signal of the end of their employment due to profitability for employers. Hence, practices related to older workers' earning partially contribute to the high cost of hiring older people.

Moreover, although pensions are fading from the equation of labor cost for employers, practices related to older workers' earnings and health insurance cost still worry employers. Employers' willingness to hire or retain older employees depends on availability of their labor, level of their productivity, and associated costs (Committee for Economic Development, 1999). This is consistent with social exchange theory that emphasizes the reciprocal benefit between older people and others (Hooyman & Kiyak, 2005). Hence, unless older workers continually upgrading their skills, desirable well-paid jobs needing new technology and skills will not open to them.

4.4.5 Stereotype against Seniors

Evidence is also found that employers tend to be culturally biased against older workers and tend not to design programs to retain them (AARP, n.d.; Barth et al., 1993; Guillemar et al., 1996; Taylor & Walker, 1998; Wagner, 1998; Henkens, 2000). In addition to possible higher labor cost of hiring older people due to seniority principles and obsolete skills of many older

72

employees, older people are typically perceived in public culture as ailing, less efficient, with slow reaction, limited learning capacity, etc (Sokolovsky, 2000). All those contribute to barriers preventing hiring older people and preventing older people from seeking for training and job opportunities.

The question is whether seniors are really slower, have worse work performance, and less productive than the young. Various studies show that age is a poor indicator of work performance and the variations in performance within the same cohorts far exceed the average differences between cohorts (Human Resources Development Canada, 1999; Sterns and McDaniel, 1994). Using data on U.S. General Motor employees, Florida State University Psychology Department and Pepper Institute on Aging and Public Policy have found that older workers are not less productive or valuable in the workplace, despite their longer learning processes (Charness, 2004). Even for the new skills related to high technology, research also shows that seniors' deficiencies in computer skills, for example, are really a function of socially driven motivation (Friedberg, 2003; Resnick et al., 2004).

Lawton and Nahemow's (1973) Competence Model can be used to explain this phenomenon. This model is composed of environmental press and individual competence. Environmental press refers to social and physical environments; individual competence refers to the theoretical upper limit of an individual's adaptability to environmental change[23]. Older adults still have the ability to learn new technologies and gain further skills. The key to this is how much the social environment facilitates and encourages them to learn these skills. Once older people learn new skills, their individual competence improves and they can handle a higher level of environmental press.

If the society generally doubts elders' learning capacity and discourages them to learn, or if the new technology and skills are totally disconnected with older people's original skill base, older people sense a strong environmental press, which may prevent older people from updating

---

[23] With a too high environmental press surpassing individual competence, individuals experience excessive stress or overload; with a too low environmental press, individuals experience sensory derivation, boredom, learned helpless, and thus depend on others (Hooyman and Kiyak, 2005).

their skills; however, if elders are encouraged to learn or the new skills and technology are related to their original skills, older people sense a limited environmental press and their individual competence can lead them to learn. If older people are total disengaged from working responsibilities and there is no need to learn new skills while they are still in good shape, they will face too low environmental press and feel bored or become dependent on others. Hence, creating a comfortable learning environment that encourages elders to learn is helpful; disengaging older people while they are still competent for many jobs will possibly either reduce their life satisfaction due to boredom or make them dependent on others due to learned helplessness resulting from too low environmental press.

4.5 Incentives for Seniors' Employment Participation

There are also positive incentives for elders to stay in the labor force and these factors have contributed to the recent increase in older people's labor force participation rate (see Appendix 4.1). At the policy level, the work disincentives associated with Social Security are going away. Those who have reached the normal retirement age are no longer subject to an earning test. This situation allows seniors to earn any amount of income without the fear of losing Social Security benefits (Burtless and Quinn, 2000; Bruce, et al., 2000). Also, as mentioned earlier, the normal retirement age for Social Security eligibility in the United States has been raised from 65 to 67. This trend may continue to push up the average retirement age and legislative efforts to raise the initial eligible age for Social Security to beyond 62.

At the individual level, health capacity and financial needs directly provide possibility and necessity for seniors to participate in the labor force. The improved health and medical conditions for seniors physically enable them to continue working after retirement; financial reasons, such as the inability to afford retirement and fear of losing access to health insurance, encourage seniors to continue working.

At the socioeconomic level, the emergence of the "footloose" "Knowledge Economy" and an increasing public attention paid to the workforce barriers of the physically challenged, are

74

making it easier for seniors to participate in the workforce. In the "Knowledge Economy", innovative arrangements, such as more attractive part-time jobs, more flexible schedules, phased retirement opportunities, and teleworking possibilities encourage older people to postpone their retirement. The flexibility offered by the teleworking options allows seniors to tend to personal or family health-related needs and enables workers to combine employment and leisure.

Culturally, the pursuit of an imprived late life satisfaction through continuing to work provides another motivation for seniors to remain in the workforce. Seniors' human capital is also being recognized and paid increasing attention to. The following subsections give more details of the above points.

4.5.1 Improved Health Conditions

As indicated in the last section, individual decisions of later retirement are largely affected by the factors of their health, financial affordability, life satisfaction through work, etc. Health condition for older Americans generally keeps enhancing, due to improving medical care, medicine and immunization technology, living conditions, and social attention to nutrition. Over the past decades, human's health conditions are much improved and life expectancy becomes longer. Americans now live longer and healthier. Hayflick (1980)'s rectangularization of the survival curve theory captures this change. Because people are living a longer and longer life, percentage of people surviving till age 100 is approaching 100% and thus approaching the rectangular shape with which 100% of people can survive till age 100. Hayflick (1980) delineated the trend of surviving curve rectangularization according to American demographic history.

This enhanced health condition and longer life biologically makes it possible for seniors to be involved in socioeconomic activities. The biological background also guarantees seniors to enjoy their work more than before. Retirement while being physically active increases boredom to many seniors. Instead, many seniors enjoy working rather than retiring. Researches have

75

evidenced the improvements in life quality that result from continuing to work rather than retirement (AARP, n.d.)[24].

In addition, factors, such as the development of "footloose" economy and more and more public attention paid to handicapped people's accessibility and mobility, reduce physical constraints for older people to work. Since older people used to work till their 70s by the 1970s when physically demanding manufacturing industries dominated job markets, now in a less physically demanding service-dominant economy and with better health situations and living conditions, why cannot older people work longer. According to the labor force data from Bureau of Labor Statistics (BLS), over the period of 1950-1980, labor force participation rate of older people was higher and people retired later than the period of 1980-2000. Although early retirement programs and other factors have withdrawn many older people from workforce, as introduced in the previous section, health condition is generally not a key factor preventing older people from working longer, comparing the historical period before 1980.

4.5.2 Financial Incentives for Late Retirement

Financial reasons are normally a key reason for older people's decision of retirement. Those financial reasons include the need for more income, inability to afford retirement, and fear of losing access to health insurance. The 2003 random telephone survey from AARP indicated that financial concerns represented the primary reason for older people to continue working (Brown, 2003). Rix (2004) also indicate that, if seniors are physically capable of working, lacking affordability to retire and fear of losing access to health insurance will put older people to work. However, if older people continue to work just because of lacking financial support, this situation will imply that older people are forced to continue working and it will reduce older people's life satisfaction, which is inconsistent with social progress expected by Americans. The

---

[24] For example, as indicated previously, a 2002 American Association of Retired Persons (AARP) survey on the attitudes of seniors found that 76% survey seniors consider work satisfaction as the major reason to continue working; 68% chose to work because they liked being productive; and 68% of the elders worked because they felt themselves useful.

policy proposal that purports a legal retirement age as late as 67 or even 70 is not included in policy considerations of this study.

4.5.3 Cultural Incentives for Late Retirement: Old is Gold

Rather than out of financial necessity, many older people believe that work is also a source of life satisfaction, which is consistent with the promotion of "successful aging" or "productive aging". Working can not only make older people feel more productive and valuable, but also keep them active in many social relationships, particularly when older people have had established comfortable networks. Hooyman & Kiyak (2005) state that, in addition to financial need, desires to feel productive, job restructuring and contingent and temporary service jobs are other reasons making older people seek employment. A 2002 AARP survey which examined older people's working attitudes disclosed that 76% of those surveyed considered work satisfaction as the major reason to continue working; 68% chose to work because they liked being productive; 68% worked because they felt themselves useful (AARP, n.d.). Research from Committee for Economic Development (1999) also point out that psychological life satisfaction is an important reason for older people to work, in addition to their own economic status and other social factors.

Many people are recognizing the value of older people's human capital. The 2003 Human Resource Management / National Older Worker Career Center[25] Older Workers Survey identifies several reasons for hiring or retaining older workers. 2003 SHRM/NOWCC/CED Older Workers Survey identified the following reasons to hire or retain older workers: invaluable experience, established business ties, strong work ethic, loyalty to company, adding diversity of

---

25 This survey is a combination of a team effort between the Society for Human Resource Management (SHRM), National Older Worker Career Center (NOWCC) and Committee for Economic Development (CED). A sample of HR professionals was randomly selected from SHRM's membership database, which consists of more than 170,000 members. In November 2002, 2,500 randomly selected SHRM members received an e-mail invitation containing a link that directed them to the online survey. Of these, 2,143 e-mails were successfully delivered to respondents, and 428 HR professionals responded, yielding a response rate of 20%.

thoughts and approaches, and mentoring to younger workers (Collison, 2003). Jimmy Carter also concluded wisdom of older people as experience, guidance, leadership, and comfort (Peterson, 1999). Technology and skill obsolescence is a concern preventing employing older people; however, older people do have valuable human capital that younger people may not possess.

Although older people are typically associated with obsolete technology and skills, research shows that older people are not naturally disconnected from new technology; instead, it is the environment that makes older people give up accepting training for new technology and skills. Friedberg (2003) finds that not only investment in computer use makes older people retire later, but also people who planned to retire later are more likely to accept training and invest in computer use. Although marketing and training for new information and communication technologies (ICT) has focused mainly on younger people due to stereotype about older people's learning capacity, recent studies from Resnick et al (2004) demonstrate that older adults can learn to use the Internet and web use can improve elders' quality of life. As Lawton (1973)'s Competence Model can be used to explain these phenomena in the previous section, older adults still have ability to learn new technology and skills. The key is how much the social environment facilitates and encourages them to do so. In terms of new skills and technology,

Another major concern from employers or general public is that older people are perceived to be less productive than younger people, but this perception could be wrong. People's intelligence is composed of Crystallized Intelligence and Fluid Intelligence (Hooyman and Kiyak, 2005). Crystallized Intelligence is a form of acquired knowledge and is usually stable until very late life; Fluid Intelligence refers to ability to quickly solve novel problems and shows declines from the 20s or 30s (Schulz and Salthouse, 1999). Although older people may have disadvantage for fluid intelligence, they may not have disadvantage for crystallized intelligence. Thus, older people may have more difficulty than younger ones for learning brand new knowledge, but it does not necessarily mean they are less productive. Human Resources Development Canada (1999) evaluated older people aged over 45 in Canada and found that there is no significant overall difference between the job performance of older and younger workers and variations within an age group far exceed the average differences between age groups in almost every study. Although this study used a difference age definition for older people and the

78

research samples are of Canadians instead of Americans, the result still shows a possible wrong stereotype of older people in terms of their productivity. Research done by Florida State University Psychology Department and Pepper Institute on Aging and Public Policy used data from U.S. corporations such as from General Motor and found that age is not a good predictor of worker productivity: although age may make older people's learning slower and take longer, age does not make significant difference in work performance and productivity (Charness, 2004). This result is consistent with research done 10 years ago by Sterns and McDaniel (1994) who indicated that age was a poor predicator of job performance.

4.5.4 Emergence of the "Knowledge Economy" and Innovative Arrangement

Economic background is an "invisible hand" influencing the timing of retirement. Current U.S. economy has transferred from a manufacturing dominant economy to a service dominant economy. The emergence of the "Knowledge Economy" elevates the importance of mental power, reduces requirement for physical labor, is less restrictive to physical locations and thus becomes more "footloose", and generates many new technological possibilities. In the "Knowledge Economy", human capital, brainpower, and innovation become the key factor driving economic growth and physical labor becomes less important. This situation makes seniors' reduced physical labor power less disadvantageous and instead makes their cumulative working skills and knowledge more valuable in the new economy. The "Knowledge Economy" encourages innovation and entrepreneurship. The "footloose" and less physically demanding feature of the "Knowledge Economy" reduces location and physical limitations for seniors to participate in the labor force.

In this background, flexible work schedule becomes more and more possible, which offers an environmental incentive for older people to continue working. Hence, more attractive part-time jobs, more flexible schedules, phased retirement opportunities, and teleworking possibilities would encourage older people to postpone retirement because the flexibility allows for older workers' personal health related needs and also enable workers to combine employment and leisure (Herman, et. al., 2003; Rix, 2004). A national survey conducted for AARP introduces phased retirement as an approach that enables older workers to reduce their work schedules and thus prolongs their work life, particularly for the retention of skilled workers (RoperASW, 2002).

Assisted technology also makes elderly entrepreneurship more possible. With more seniors in the population and with an increasing concern about handicapped people, assisted technology has been of public focuses. Information technology further expedited the development of assisted technology by reducing geographic limitations. The assisted technology makes it more possible for seniors to work and therefore increases the ease for seniors to continue working.

4.6 Rising Seniors' Labor Force Participation

All the above incentives contribute to recent rising labor force participation of seniors. In the United States, data from Bureau of Labor Statistics (BLS) shows the upward trend over the past decade for older people's labor force participation rate and their employment-population ratio, shown in Appendix 4.1. Using random digit dialing, in 2003 AARP conducted a nationwide telephone survey of 2001 workers between the ages of 50 and 70 to explore their vision of retirement and found that majority of pre-retirees defined retirement to include some form of work (Brown, 2003). In Europe, the 'Dutch miracle' in the 1990s that changed public attitudes from negative to positive on seniors' involvement into the workforce has led to a high rate of employment growth and further stimulated early retirement reforms (van Dalen & Henkens, 2002).

Part IV Seniors' Employability in the "Knowledge Economy"

Chapter 5 Seniors' Labor Force Participation: Clues from Social Gerontology Theories[26]

The previous chapter summarized the disincentives and incentives for seniors to participate in the labor force. Is participating in the labor force beneficial to seniors? To further explore whether seniors should be involved in the labor force, this chapter attempted to seek for supporting theories and thus examines the social gerontology theories. However, these social gerontology theories present conflicting views on whether to involve the elderly in the labor force. Role theories (Cottrell, 1942) and disengagement theories (Marshall, 1994) discourage seniors' social involvement, while activity theories (Bengtson, 1969) and continuity theories encourage their involvement.

5.1 Theories against Seniors' Labor Force Participation

This stream of theories purport that seniors, as their biological ages indicate, need to adjust to their new role—being seniors, and be less active in the social and economic activities than before, to achieve their life satisfaction in late ages. Among the social gerontology theories that are against seniors' involvement in the labor force include the role theory and the disengagement theory.

---

[26] Part of the literature review in this chapter is excerpted from Zhang (2008).

5.1.1 Role Theory

The role theory is one of the earliest theories explaining how individuals adjust to aging (Cottrell, 1942). According to this theory, individuals play a variety of social roles that vary with their ages[27] or stages of life. At each stage in life, the roles reflect social being and offer the basis of their self-concept. Age norms control the roles that individuals play and they operate informally in society. The age norm is also often an individual's measure of the appropriateness of their behavior. In this context, Hagestad and Neugarten (1985) note that social clocks become internalized and age norms operate to keep people on the time track. The age norm is conveyed by socialization and thus, most people in the U.S. society have age-normative expectations of the roles.

Based on this theory, older people are expected to withdraw from the labor force based on social norms and consequently, take on the role of retirement. The change of roles sometimes also equates with role discontinuity. That may be why some newly retired seniors feel bored and experience a dramatic decline in life satisfaction. In this case, there is a conflict between social expectation and individual life satisfaction. Social expectation is for seniors to take their role, but some seniors' individual perception is that the "seniors' role" increases boredom. However, this theory believes that in the long run, when seniors are used to taking their "seniors' role", their life satisfaction will increase.

5.1.2 Disengagement Theory

The disengagement theory looks at the social system, rather than just individuals, as an explanation for successful adjustment to aging (Hooyman and Kiyak, 2005). According to this theory, older people experience reduced activity levels and tend to interact less frequently with others. This situation leads them to seek more passive roles and to become preoccupied with their inner lives. Disengagement is thus viewed as adaptive behavior that justifies older people's

---

[27] Mostly chronological ages, sometimes biological or psychological ages.

loss of occupational roles. This theory challenges the assumption of activity theory[28] and views older age as a separate period of life, not as an extension of middle age.

Disengagement theory is the first real comprehensive, explicit, and multidisciplinary theory on social gerontology (Achenbaum and Bengtson, 1994), but it has many limitations. The disengagement theory, although attempting to explain both system-and individual-level changes with one grand theory, has not found empirical supports (Achenbaum and Bengtson, 1994). With better health and increased longevity, a growing number of seniors remain in the labor force. Similar to previous theories, disengagement theory also fails to account for variations in individual preferences, personality, socio-cultural settings, and environmental opportunities as factors influencing older people's life (Achenbaum and Bengtson, 1994; Marshall, 1994; Estes and Associates, 2000). As Hooyman and Kiyak (2005) have noted, it cannot be assumed that older people's withdrawal from useful roles is necessarily good for society or for older people. For example, policies to encourage retirement that have been implemented in the past resulted in the loss of older workers' skills and knowledge in the workplace. This is an increasingly critical issue, especially during periods of employees' skill shortages along with an aging workforce.

5.2 Theories Supporting Seniors' Labor Force Participation

Not all social gerontology theories that support reducing seniors' labor force participation. Instead, there are also social gerontology theories that are in support of seniors' involvement in the labor force as well as other social activities. Those theories are represented by the activity theory and the continuity theory.

5.2.1 Activity Theory

The activity theory views aging to a large degree as an extension of the middle age. According to this theory, the more active an older person is, the greater their life satisfaction,

---

[28] The activity theory will be introduced in the following section.

positive self-concept, and adjustment to the aging process can be (Bengtson, 1969). Activity theory thus encourages the integration of seniors into society. Therefore, seniors who stay in the labor force or keep productive as entrepreneurs are expected to enhance positive self-concept. Hooyman and Kiyak (2005) also show evidence that a person's experience with the aging process is more positive if they remain engaged in the workplace.

Activity theory, however, fails to consider other variables, such as personality, lifestyle, and socioeconomic status, when addressing the relationship between activity level and well being, as Covey (1981) indicates. The level of older people's activeness is not the only factor determining their positive self-concept. Other factors may play an important role.

5.2.2 Continuity Theory

The continuity theory focuses on the social-psychological theories of adaptation. Similar to activity theory, continuity theory purports that individuals tend to maintain a consistent pattern of behavior as they age and their life satisfaction is determined by how consistent their current activities or lifestyles are with their lifetime experiences (Atchley, 1972; Neugarten, et al., 1968). This theory is consistent with the empirical finding that seniors with previous entrepreneurial experience or experience in white-collar manager occupations are more likely to venture into entrepreneurship around the retirement age (Fuch, 1982). Like many other gerontology theories, however, continuity theory overlooks the role of external social and environmental factors during the process of aging.

5.3 Other Related Social Gerontology Theories

Different from the above theories, there are a few other theoretical perspectives that place more emphasis on the macro-level and structural analysis. Those theoretical perspectives include the interactionist theory, political economy of aging, and social phenomenologists and social constructionists.

The interactionist theory interprets the person-environment transaction process and emphasizes the dynamic interaction between older individuals and the social environment (Hooyman and Kiyak, 2005). The theory purports that the dynamic social world shapes older people's perceptions, decisions, behavior, etc., and older individuals also change the ongoing social environment (including policies, culture, social biases, economic environment, etc). Over time, older people's occupational choices are expected to change. Various socioeconomic factors interact with an older individual's experience in terms of aging and affect their decisions regarding employment.

Political economy of aging theory emphasizes the socioeconomic and political constraints that shape older people's experience. According to this theory, socioeconomic class is a structural barrier to older people's access to social resources; more dominant groups perpetuate class inequalities (Olson, 1982; Minkler and Estes, 1984; Overbo and Minkler, 1993). In a capitalized society, the socioeconomic and political constraints that are socially constructed play an important role in older individuals' employment decisions.

The social phenomenologists and social constructionist theory also address the socioeconomic environment as an important source shaping older individuals' attitudes and behavior. This theory argues that individual behavior shaped by social definitions and social structures produces a "reality" (Ray, 1996), or a fact and environment, which in turn structures individuals' lives (Bengtson et. al., 1997). The following chart (Figure 5.1) summarize the above social gerontology theories.

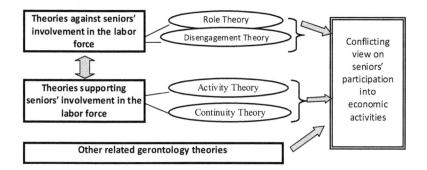

Figure 5.1 Social Gerontology Theories

Source: adapted from Zhang (2008).

Chapter 6 Seniors in the Labor Force: Senior Workers' Industry Mix

Chapter 5 introduced the social gerontology theories that are related to the debate on seniors' labor force participation. It would be interesting to quickly examine the industry sector distribution of senior workers and find out what sectors senior workers tend to be concentrated in. This chapter therefore attempts to empirically explore whether the "Knowledge Economy" is suitable for older people to participate the workforce. The empirical exploration in this chapter relies on available data issued in the *Profiles of Older Workers in 2004/ 2005*, partnered between the 12 states and the Census Bureau Local Employment Dynamics. The reason to use this dataset to examine the labor force participation status and industry mix is that this dataset offers direct information needed for this chapter. For a quick and preliminary comparison, this dataset serves well. Although this dataset defines seniors differently from several later chapters that relies on the Public Use Micro Sample data by referring to those who are aged 65 and above, using a different dataset in this chapter not only serves a preliminary exploration purpose, but also avoid the heavy reliance on one dataset that might have potential bias.

However, it is worth noting that this data set has a few limitations. Firstly, data at regional level only covers the limited 12 states and only 11 states can be used for comparison because data of California was of a different year (2001) from the rest 11 states (2002). Secondly, the industry code used in those reports is not consistent with NAICS code. Without conversion explanation between this industry code and NAICS, it is impossible to compare with other standard data sources that cover national data. The major sectors included in these reports are (1) agriculture, (2) mining, (3) construction, (4) manufacturing, (5) transportation, communication, and utilities, (4) wholesale trade, (5) retail trade, (6) financial, insurance, real estate (FIRE), and (7) services.

88

According to this classification, services, FIRE, and retail trade are relatively related to the "Knowledge Economy". Thus, this chapter will focus on these three sectors. Thirdly, the state level regional data are normally not as good as metropolitan data for employment analysis. State boundaries are arbitrary and political, while employment boundaries tend to be more relevant to metropolitan boundaries. Since other regional data on older people's employment are not available at this moment, the data, though limited, is used to generate simple spatial analysis.

This chapter uses four proportion comparisons for analysis. Comparing those proportions can delineate a state's specialized industries. Those proportions can also generate location quotients that can describe a state's industry mix. The detailed proportion calculations will be introduced with their results. In this chapter, we call states that have a higher proportion of seniors among its population "older states". Those older states also tend to have an older median age for its population. To find out whether the older states have a bigger proportion of older workers among total employment across industry sectors, those 11 states are ranked according to the proportion of elders among the total state population. Geographic Information System (GIS) is used to mapping the U.S. Census 2000 data according to geocodes of the corresponding states, as shown in Figure 6.1. Figure 6.2 displays the percentage of older people and the median ages of those states.

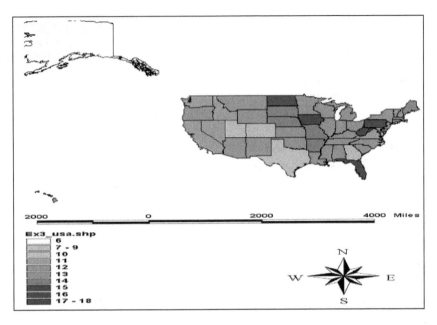

Figure 6.1 Percentages of Older People among Total State Population in 2000

Source: U.S. Census Bureau 2000.

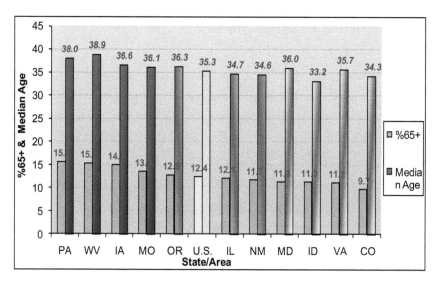

Figure 6.2 Age Structure of Selected States
Source: U.S. Census Bureau 2000.

Although data are not available for all states, the listed 11 states possibly compose an acceptable sample of the U.S. states. The proportion of older people among the total U.S. population in 2000 is 12.4%, and the 11 states represent a balanced variance of this national mean. The listed 11 states include 4 states with a high concentration of older people: Pennsylvania, West Virginia, Iowa, and Missouri; 3 states with a medium proportion of older people: Oregon, Illinois, New Mexico; 4 states representing low concentration of seniors: Maryland, Virginia, Idaho, and Colorado. Those 11 states also disperse into different regions in the United States: East, North, Middle West, and South. Although the 11 states are not randomly selected sample for the U.S. states, they can at least represent a big proportion of states in this country in terms of older people's distribution.

6.1 Industry Distribution of Older Workers

To test whether the "Knowledge Economy" is more suitable for older people to work, this chapter first examines what industries older people are concentrated in. Particularly it would be necessary to see whether older workers tend to concentrate into services, Finance, Insurance, and Real Estate (FIRE), and retail trade, instead of the other industries that are labor intensive and the core industries in the 'Fordist economy'. Figure 6.3 presents the result of the first proportion in this chapter:

Number of older workers in *industry i* in state j

Total number of older workers across *all industries* in state j.

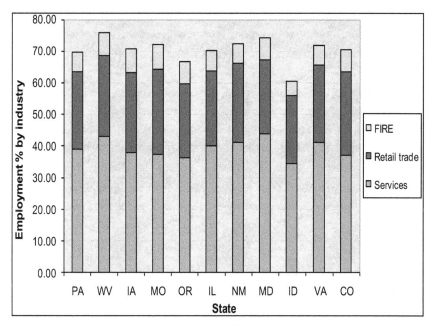

Figure 6.3 Industry Distribution of Older Workers in Selected States in 2002
Data source: the *Profiles of Older Workers in 2004/ 2005.*

This above proportion describes the proportion of an industry/sector's share in a state's total seniors' employment and therefore indicates whether this state has a relatively higher concentration of this sector, compared to other states. The following three paragraphs present the results reflected from this proportion.

 *Services take a **dominant** proportion of older people's employment* across the 11 states. Averagely around 40% of older workers in those 11 states work in service industries. States close to the Greater Washington Metropolitan area, such as Maryland, Virginia, and West Virginia have a higher percentage of older workers in service industries, which is consistent with the economic transition from industries for goods to industries for services in the Greater Washington Metropolitan area.

Retail and FIRE also take a significant percentage of older workers. *The three "Knowledge Economy" related sectors—services, retail trade, and FIRE totally take around 70% of older workers.* Although a smaller percentage of older workers in Idaho than that in other states participate in those three service-related sectors, these three sectors still take more than 60% of older workers in Idaho.

Across these 11 states, the percentages of older people among the total state population seem not related to how older workers are distributed in terms of industries (r < = 0.3, shown in Table 7.1); however, *the state median ages seem to positively correlate with older workers' concentration into those three "Knowledge Economy" related sectors* (r > = 0.4, shown in Table 7.1), particularly with those three sectors as a whole (r= 0. 57, shown in Table 7.1). The positive correlations indicate that *the older a state's median age, the bigger the proportion of older workers participating in the sectors of services, retail trade, and FIRE.* However, since the sample size in this analysis is too small (n=11), this result needs to be further verified.

Table 6.1 Older Workers in the Service-related Industries

State	Med age	% older	Service	Retail	FIRE	Sum (S.R.F)
West Virginia	38.9	15.3	42.86	25.74	7.14	75.74
Pennsylvania	38.0	15.6	38.86	24.51	6.15	69.52
Iowa	36.6	14.9	37.77	25.43	7.43	70.63
Oregon	36.3	12.8	36.19	23.49	7.12	66.79
Missouri	36.1	13.5	37.41	26.89	7.70	71.99
Maryland	36.0	11.3	43.68	23.54	6.91	74.14
Virginia	35.7	11.2	41.08	24.58	6.20	71.85
Illinois	34.7	12.1	39.92	23.68	6.65	70.25
New Mexico	34.6	11.7	41.17	25.03	6.02	72.23
Colorado	34.3	9.7	36.95	26.53	6.93	70.41
Idaho	33.2	11.3	34.37	21.46	4.74	60.57
Corr w % older	0.83		0.10	0.22	0.33	0.22
Corr w Med age		0.83	0.44	0.38	0.51	0.57

6.2 Industries that are more Senior-Friendly

Although the above findings present that older workers are relatively concentrated in the sectors of services, retail trade, and even FIRE, compared with other industrial sectors, it is difficult to tell whether older workers are more specialized in those three sectors, compared with younger workers. The following proportion compares older people's employment with the total state employment across sectors, calculated as follows:

Number of *older* workers in industry i in state j

Number of *all* workers in industry i in state j.

The available data defined the total employment as employment of people aged 14 and above. Figure 6.4 delineates the proportion of older workers among total employment across sectors. To make the figure easy to read and also to indicate the importance of the "Knowledge Economy", only proportions in the major knowledge-economy-associated three sectors are included. As shown in this figure, the curve indicating services is always above the curve indicating all-industry average. Hence, *among the total employment, there are a higher percentage of older workers in services than in the all-industry average.* For the economy of the 11 states, services hire more senior workers than the average of all industries. Although the curve of retail trade tends to be above the curve of all-industry average for 9 of the 11 states, this trend is not evident for New Mexico and Idaho. FIRE shows only a slight advantage over the curve of all-industry average for 4 states. *Relative to the sectoral total employment across all the 11 states, services have the highest percentage of older workers and thus are most elderly friendly.*

95

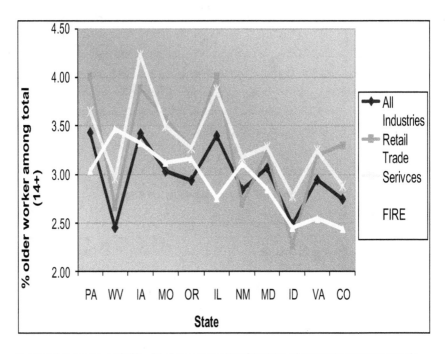

Figure 6.4 Percentage of Older Workers among Total State Employment by Major Sectors in 2002

6.3 Comparison across the 11 States—Location Quotients

So far, according to the limited data, older workers seem to concentrate and specialize in services. Since services represent the trend of the "Knowledge Economy", older people seem to show a consistency with the development of the "Knowledge Economy". If this is further verified with a larger database, developing the "Knowledge Economy" could attract more seniors into the workforce and older people have the potential to be more involved into the workforce in the service-focused "Knowledge Economy" than the manufacturing-focused "Fordist economy".

To compare the interstate differences across the 11 states and to investigate regional industry mix trends, the location quotient analysis is used. Since national employment data by age cannot be used because of different industry classifications for data integration, this paper uses the sum of the 11 states as the entire study area for the calculation of location quotients. The first location quotient is to identify which sector is more specialized by older people in the 11 states. The location quotients are thus calculated as

LQ_1= [number of older workers in ***industry i*** of **state j** / number of older workers in ***all industries*** of **state j]** / [number of older workers in ***industry i*** of **all 11 states** / number of older workers in ***all industries*** of **all 11 states**]

Table 6.2 presents the location quotients. Compared with the mean value of the 11 states, the 3 major sectors—retail trade, FIRE, and services—develop in balance in the 11 states, with location quotients around 1. Relative to the 11-state mean, Idaho displays slight weakness in all the three major sectors, which indicates that older workers in Idaho slightly specialize in traditional industries other than retail trade, FIRE, and services. In terms of sub-sectors, ***extremely high location quotients are typically concentrated in services***, as highlighted in Table 6.2. For example, older workers in Pennsylvania are specialized in educational services; older workers in West Virginia are specialized in personal services, miscellaneous repair services, and private households; older workers in Oregon are highly specialized in membership organizations; New Mexican and Idaho older workers are highly specialized in unclassified services; Virginian older workers are highly specialized in private households, museums, galleries, and gardens. FIRE also has a few high location quotients. In the meantime, also as highlighted in Table 6.2, ***the extremely low location quotients also lie in some Service and FIRE sectors***. Thus, ***while older workers concentrate in services and FIRE, this concentration is selective for sub-sectors in services and FIRE.***

Table 6.2 Location Quotients for Older Workers by Industry by State
97

	PA	WV	IA	MO	OR	IL	NM	MD	VA	ID	CO
Retail trade	1.00	1.05	1.03	1.09	0.95	0.96	1.02	0.96	1.00	*0.87*	1.08
Building	0.95	1.27	1.17	1.11	0.82	0.96	0.97	0.92	0.94	1.23	1.21
General	1.02	1.15	1.11	1.30	0.64	0.87	1.20	0.87	1.02	0.97	1.15
Food	1.31	1.12	1.06	0.94	0.69	0.94	0.67	0.89	1.10	0.91	0.46
Car	1.06	1.20	1.33	1.44	1.07	0.77	0.97	0.86	0.95	0.92	0.93
Apparel	1.07	1.02	1.02	0.94	0.91	1.00	1.10	1.20	0.90	0.83	0.80
Home	0.89	1.24	1.12	0.94	0.96	0.92	1.28	1.08	1.22	1.20	0.99
Eating	0.74	0.76	0.79	0.92	1.31	1.23	1.03	0.92	0.93	0.70	**1.50**
Miscellaneous	1.06	1.06	0.99	1.06	0.93	0.84	1.09	1.17	1.03	0.76	1.08
FIRE	0.92	1.07	1.12	1.16	1.07	1.00	0.91	1.04	0.93	*0.71*	1.04
Depository	1.03	1.28	1.48	1.15	*0.43*	1.26	0.73	0.64	0.73	*0.44*	0.80
Nondepository	0.61	0.71	0.94	0.94	1.08	1.04	1.01	1.36	1.27	0.76	**1.52**
Security	0.98	***0.36***	0.66	1.35	*0.59*	1.22	0.65	1.06	0.80	*0.54*	1.03
Insur. Carrier	1.15	0.50	1.35	1.03	*0.54*	1.19	0.85	0.82	0.68	0.66	0.80
Insur. Agents	0.96	**1.51**	1.29	1.08	1.01	1.07	0.86	0.89	0.81	0.98	0.87
Real	0.82	1.14	0.91	1.21	1.61	0.76	1.02	1.32	1.13	0.82	1.22
Holding/other	0.96	0.72	0.99	1.10	1.23	0.99	1.34	0.91	0.90	0.65	1.23
Service	0.99	1.09	0.96	0.95	0.92	1.01	1.05	1.11	1.04	*0.87*	0.94
Hotels/other	0.78	1.32	1.02	1.11	1.51	0.72	**1.75**	0.70	1.21	1.39	**1.78**
Personal	0.83	**1.78**	1.03	1.32	*0.57*	0.83	0.77	1.20	**1.47**	0.69	0.86
Business	0.77	0.73	0.80	0.78	0.89	1.31	0.95	1.09	1.09	0.99	1.06
Car	0.87	0.87	0.96	1.05	1.01	0.94	1.03	0.97	1.06	**1.56**	1.44
Miscellaneous	0.82	**1.82**	0.96	0.86	0.74	0.98	1.03	1.16	1.28	1.25	1.10
Motion	0.91	1.02	0.77	0.68	1.38	1.19	1.56	1.07	0.93	0.81	0.93
Amusement	1.08	1.18	1.12	1.19	0.78	0.85	0.70	1.11	0.91	0.79	1.14
Health	1.06	1.30	1.25	1.04	0.76	1.02	1.02	1.02	0.86	0.81	0.79
Legal	1.11	1.34	0.95	0.93	0.77	1.01	1.12	1.00	0.98	*0.58*	0.88
Educational	**1.68**	0.37	0.84	0.69	0.60	0.98	*0.46*	1.19	0.65	*0.29*	0.47
Social	0.99	1.42	1.16	1.08	1.08	0.95	1.26	1.07	0.85	1.17	0.85
Museums,	1.08	***0.30***	0.97	0.65	0.76	0.80	0.94	0.76	**2.24**	*0.53*	0.62
Membership	1.20	1.25	0.72	0.77	**2.31**	0.95	0.81	0.88	0.83	*0.50*	0.79
Engineering,	0.87	0.71	*0.50*	0.67	0.65	0.95	**1.72**	**1.72**	1.42	0.80	1.00
Private	0.67	**1.71**	0.65	**1.45**	0.69	0.60	1.15	**1.49**	**2.31**	*0.58*	*0.40*
Services (uncl.)	0.87	0.78	*0.19*	1.25	0.95	1.15	**2.43**	0.91	*0.51*	2.03	**1.53**

To compare older workers with younger workers, location quotients representing percentages of older workers among all workers in each industry of each state are calculated as follow:

LQ_2 = [number of *older workers* in industry i of **state j** / number of *all-age total employment* in industry i of **state j**] / [number of *older workers* in industry i of **all 11 states** / number of *all-age total employment* in industry i of **all 11 states**]

Table 6.3 displays the results. As shown in Table 6.3, compared with location quotients on all industries as a whole, location quotients on services are typically higher in 7 states; among the rest 4 states, Colorado, Pennsylvania, and Maryland have higher location quotients on either retail trade or FIRE than the locations quotients on all-industry average; Idaho has the same location quotient on services as on all industries as a whole. Thus, *at least one of the three knowledge-economy-associated sectors tend to be more specialized in hiring older workers than all-industry average across all the 11 states*. Moreover, Table 6.3 shows that several "younger states"[29], such as New Mexico, Maryland, Virginia, Idaho, and Colorado, have location quotients on all-industry-total employment below 1; in the meantime, several "older states", such as Pennsylvania and Iowa, have location quotients on all-industry-total employment above 1. *This situation that "older states" have a higher proportion of elders among all-industry-total employment indicates that older people are not just dependents in those states; they also work to support the state economy*. Among the 11 states, compared with younger workers, older workers' specializations differ across states: in Iowa, elders show a high specialization in several FIRE sectors, West Virginian older workers show a high specialization in personal services and unclassified services, New Mexican and Idaho older workers show a high specialization in holding or other investment offices, and Virginian older workers show a strong specialization in private households services and museum, galleries, and gardens.

---

[29] "Younger states" means states with a lower proportion of older people or lower median age than the national average; and "older states" means states with a higher proportion of older people or higher median age than the national average. Table 6.3 has ordered the 11 states in terms of age from the left to the right.

Table 6.3 Location Quotients for Older Workers among Total Employment by Industry by State

	PA	WV	IA	MO	OR	IL	NM	MD	VA	ID	CO
INDUSTRY ALL	1.09	*0.78*	1.08	0.96	0.93	1.08	0.90	0.97	0.93	*0.79*	0.87
Retail trade	1.12	0.75	1.09	1.00	0.92	1.12	0.76	0.90	0.90	*0.63*	0.92
Building	1.09	0.92	1.10	1.04	0.84	1.16	0.69	0.89	0.96	0.67	0.84
General	1.17	0.75	1.07	1.09	0.63	1.07	0.77	0.96	0.83	0.65	1.07
Food	1.24	0.77	1.08	1.03	0.69	1.10	0.62	0.78	0.96	0.58	0.63
Car	1.34	0.71	1.04	1.09	0.88	1.01	0.66	0.84	0.90	0.63	0.81
Apparel	1.06	0.95	1.35	1.09	0.91	1.07	1.03	0.92	0.82	0.92	0.79
Home	1.19	1.32	1.28	0.99	0.85	1.00	1.04	0.95	0.92	0.82	0.74
Eating	0.89	0.54	0.89	0.79	1.25	1.42	0.71	0.90	0.86	0.52	1.12
Miscellaneous	1.11	0.88	1.27	1.11	0.99	0.91	0.93	1.01	0.93	0.74	0.92
FIRE	1.06	1.21	1.16	1.09	1.10	0.96	1.08	0.99	0.89	0.85	0.85
Depository	1.06	0.99	**1.53**	1.14	0.51	1.17	0.71	0.74	0.73	0.43	0.80
Nondepository	1.16	1.02	0.83	0.90	0.98	1.19	1.06	1.08	0.71	1.11	1.11
Security	1.37	1.24	**1.80**	0.82	1.03	0.88	1.53	0.89	1.14	1.11	0.81
Insur. Carrier	1.13	1.04	0.99	1.10	0.69	1.03	1.61	1.01	0.79	0.96	0.71
Insur. Agents	0.99	0.97	1.04	1.03	0.85	1.07	0.95	0.90	1.11	0.86	0.88
Real	1.15	1.36	**1.58**	1.13	1.16	0.90	1.00	0.91	0.88	0.92	0.78
Holding/other	0.74	1.17	**1.98**	1.13	1.86	1.04	**2.00**	1.13	1.18	**1.73**	0.67
Service	1.04	0.84	1.21	1.00	0.94	1.11	0.91	0.94	0.93	0.79	0.82
Hotels/other	1.07	0.80	1.16	1.09	1.23	1.03	0.87	0.82	0.91	0.85	0.99
Personal	0.93	**1.48**	1.20	1.23	0.73	0.91	0.80	0.98	1.20	0.71	0.76
Business	1.09	0.85	1.13	0.89	1.01	1.30	0.96	0.85	0.76	0.96	0.77
Car	1.02	0.85	1.20	0.93	0.92	1.01	0.90	0.84	1.03	1.17	1.12
Miscellaneous	1.05	0.81	1.00	0.91	0.74	1.09	0.80	1.08	1.11	0.85	0.85
Motion	1.28	0.98	1.03	0.66	0.89	1.20	1.35	1.00	0.84	0.70	0.63
Amusement	1.25	0.81	1.20	0.98	0.88	0.99	0.79	1.05	0.93	0.67	0.70
Health	0.96	0.71	1.34	1.00	0.79	1.13	0.96	0.98	0.97	0.76	0.87
Legal	1.11	0.90	1.68	0.96	0.73	0.95	1.07	1.06	0.97	0.63	0.82
Educational	1.10	0.75	1.11	0.83	0.76	1.07	0.88	0.91	0.92	0.65	0.71
Social	0.90	0.88	1.20	1.11	0.82	1.18	0.86	0.88	1.08	0.85	0.94
Museums,	1.25	0.92	1.79	0.74	0.76	0.66	1.33	0.78	**1.48**	1.63	0.71
Membership	1.23	1.11	0.94	0.95	1.21	0.91	1.23	1.10	0.70	0.73	0.85
Engineering,	1.12	0.87	1.16	1.00	0.90	1.07	0.88	1.06	0.94	0.59	0.79
Private	0.86	1.17	1.24	1.02	0.94	0.99	1.01	0.86	**2.31**	0.72	0.61
Services (uncl.)	0.78	**1.69**	0.59	0.95	1.29	1.12	**1.68**	1.47	0.51	0.91	1.09

6.4 Limitation of This Empirical Study and Future Research

As emphasized earlier, data limitation is the first constraint that affects the effectiveness of the findings. First, the data are only one-year cross sectional data in 2002. With only one-year data, the comparison between the "Fordist economy" and the "Knowledge Economy" cannot reflect the changes and trends. Second, the sample size is too small and samples of the States are not randomly selected. The 11 states are the only data available at this moment. Although the 11 states have a certain representative power in terms of seniors' distribution, they cannot totally explain the economy of the whole United States. Thirdly, the industry classification is not clear and thus difficult to directly indicate the "Fordist economy" versus the "Knowledge Economy". This situation weakens the validity of the findings that were attempted to associate with the "Knowledge Economy" and prevents integrating with other datasets for further study.

This empirical study only uses basic data presentation. When more data are available, further research using more systematic methods would be necessary. Also, "services" is a very vague and general term. It is necessary to further investigate what level of services are older people concentrated in, i.e., whether those senior-concentrated services are the value-added services or low-level services. This classification is important for the implication of senior-related economic policy. At this stage, the limited data source does not allow distinguishing different levels of services. To further investigate this issue, better data and deeper investigation would be critical.

6.5 Conclusion and Policy Implications

The "Knowledge Economy" related sectors, such as services, FIRE, and even retail trade, seem to be more elderly friendly. The empirical analysis across 11 states in the United States shows that older workers are more concentrated in the three knowledge-economy-associated sectors, particularly in services; however, this concentration is selective in the sub-sectors. Across sectors, services tend to have the highest proportion of senior workers, and at least one of the three knowledge-economy-associated sectors tend to be more specialized in hiring older workers than all-industry average across all the 11 states. The significant positive correlation between states'

101

median age and senior workers' concentration into the three sectors indicate that the older a state's median age is, the larger the proportion of older workers in the sectors of services, retail trade, and FIRE tend to be. The situation that "older states" have a higher proportion of senior workers indicates that seniors are not just dependents in those state, they also work to support the state economy. However, due to the limitations of the data, this empirical test needs to be further tested and supported.

Based on the above analysis, the "Knowledge Economy" is possibly more suitable for older people to work than the "Fordist economy". If further empirical tests with better datasets are done, this finding may generate important policy implications: the current economic shift from the "Fordist economy" to the "Knowledge Economy" generates more opportunities for older people to join the workforce; involving more seniors into the workforce may possibly push the economy to efficiently grow.

If senior workers' economic role were true and important in the "Knowledge Economy", encouraging more seniors to participate in the labor force would not only benefit the economy, but also ease many worries, concerns, and even crises resulted from population aging. Seniors themselves, if be treated well and work pleasantly, would enhance their life satisfaction.

This chapters serves as a preliminary and exploratory study for seniors workers' sector concentration. Considering the limitation of this research, the following chapters therefore further investigate seniors' economic role, as well as labor and fiscal roles. Before that, the first worthy digging question would be whether age is a major factor prohibiting seniors to participate in the labor force and whether seniors are not suitable to be an active member of the economic society.

To investigate whether seniors can take an active role in the economy, this following chapter starts with investigating the age effect on seniors occupation behavior. Considering the fact that entrepreneurship is a key drive of the "Knowledge Economy" and entrepreneurship is often considered a phenomenon and attribute of the young, the following few chapter focus on exploring the role of seniors' entrepreneurship. If seniors could even succeed in entrepreneurship and age was not an obstacle for entrepreneurship, how would age hinder seniors' from taking responsibilities in wage-and-salary jobs? Chapter 7 therefore starts with examining the sectors seniors' employment tend to fall in, based on a different dataset. Then this chapter investigates whether older age is negatively related to seniors' labor force participation.

102

Chapter 7 Age and Seniors' Occupations[30]

Younger people are often believed not only to be more likely to generate new ideas and more likely to take risks, but also often believed to be more productive than their older counterparts. In the United States, some Americans unfortunately do not give a very positive attitude toward seniors and the process of aging becomes a sort of taboo for those people. When talking about entrepreneurship, magazines and newspaper typically focus on young entrepreneurs: being young becomes an asset and the fact of being young itself possess a natural marketing power to attract venture capital and social attention. Some venture capital even aims at young college students and there are numerous college student business plan competitions. However, have any of these efforts focused on seniors? Although population aging has been a heatedly discussed social concern, seniors are basically addressed to be a social burden that causes problems. In some rare occasions even when seniors are recognized as contributor to the economy, it is normally due to their contribution to consumption that stimulates the economy. Very little literature addresses seniors as a valuable asset that directly achieves entrepreneurship and creates productivity in the economy.

In the "Knowledge Economy", is age a factor affecting seniors' occupational choice? Are seniors who have reached retirement age less likely to be entrepreneurs, compared to the younger ones? This chapter examines how the age of an individual affects their occupation sector choice and whether seniors have a positive propensity to be entrepreneurs.

Previous literature projects a vague shadow on the relationship between age and occupational choice. A conventional view holds that seniors are not as entrepreneurial as the

---

[30] The data analysis parts of this chapter, particularly on the self-employment and entrepreneurship, are adapted from Zhang (2008).

103

young and seniors are less likely to start a new firm. The global research on entrepreneurship by the Global Entrepreneurship Monitor (GEM) (2001, 2004) noted that people aged 55-64 tend to be less entrepreneurial than the younger working-age groups because seniors have a lower scale of Total Entrepreneurial Activity (TEA) opportunities, TEA necessity, the quantity of nascent firms and entrepreneurship prevalence. Johnson (1978) and Miller (1984) justify this conventional view by a risk factor—they purport that younger workers, compared to older workers, tend to try riskier occupations first.

The opposite view on the relationship between age and occupational choice purports that seniors, compared to the younger ones, have a higher self-employment or a higher entrepreneurial propensity. An empirical study in the United States and Canada indicated the existence of a higher self-employment rate among seniors than among the younger cohorts (Reardon, 1997). Blanchflower et al. (2001) also find in their cross-country study a higher proportion of seniors than of younger people are actually self-employed, though a higher proportion of younger people prefer to be self-employed. The stronger preference for self-employment among the young could be due to several reasons including psychological ones.

There also exists a neutral view on the relationship between age and entrepreneurship. Evans and Leighton (1989) suggest that the probability of choosing self-employment is roughly independent of age. To be more specific, the fraction of the self-employed labor force increases with age until the early 40s and then remains constant until the retirement years.

In terms of theories, social gerontology theories (see Chapter 5) do not make a clear conclusion whether seniors should be involved in the economic activity or not. Role theory and disengagement theories discourage seniors to be involved in active economic activities and entrepreneurship because seniors, as well as other people of other ages, should accept their age characteristics and adjust to the role of their corresponding age. This stream of theories believes that by learning how to adjust people's behavior to the social role of that age, seniors can achieve a higher amount of happiness. On the other hand, active theory and continuity theory purports a more active life for seniors. This stream of theories believe that happiness in the late life come from active retirement life and continuing to do what they are used to do before.

104

This chapter attempts to reveal the mystery of the relationship between age and occupation choice. Specifically, three questions are investigated: first, whether individuals older than the average retirement age (62 currently in the United States) are more likely than younger people to be self-employed[31]; second, whether those seniors' self-employment tends to be more concentrated in the knowledge-based sectors than younger individuals' self-employment; third, whether elderly workers who are aged 62 are more likely than their younger counterparts to become entrepreneurs.

The analysis presented in this book uses some specific definitions for the "Knowledge Economy", the elderly, and entrepreneurship. As a quick review of the definitions in Part I, the *"Knowledge Economy"* is measured by employment in the "creative class" (Florida, 2004). The *elderly* are defined as those aged 62 and above. In the United States, 62 is the average retirement age (Gendell, 2001) and the initial eligibility age for Social Security. The younger cohort is defined as individuals between the age of 16 and 61, considering the fact that 16 is the starting age for labor force participation.

Entrepreneurship is defined in this book's empirical tests as unincorporated and incorporated self-employment rates in knowledge-based occupations. Part I of this book first introduces the original theoretical meaning of entrepreneurship—such as innovation and defining new markets. When entrepreneurship is used in empirical modeling since this chapter, entrepreneurship is measured as knowledge-based unincorporated and incorporate self-employment[32]. According to other studies, particularly in the elderly entrepreneurship literature, self-employment is a best-available measure for entrepreneurship (Evans and Leighton, 1989; Blanchflower et al., 2001). The measure of entrepreneurship that is employed in this book, i.e.

---

[31] Observations of the very old ages (in the upper 80s or 90s) would possibly be dropped due to their different behavior patterns from others.

[32] This book tries to incorporate several important components of entrepreneurship that are applicable to the elderly. Those components include: innovation entrepreneurship and business organization (Baumol, 1993) and opportunity entrepreneurship and necessarily entrepreneurship (Reynolds et. al. 2005). Innovation entrepreneurship emphasizes the innovation and high technology focus of entrepreneurship. Business organization recognizes the organizational skills as a necessary part of entrepreneurship. Opportunity entrepreneurship is defined as a new business that is set up to pursue an opportunity. Necessity entrepreneurship is defined as a start-up that occurs because of missing alternatives (e.g., out of unemployment).

the knowledge-based incorporated and unincorporated self-employment, is therefore the best available proxy measure to entrepreneurship. Although there are drawbacks of using self-employment as a measure for entrepreneurship, as discussed in Zhang (2008), using knowledge-based unincorporated and incorporated self-employment to measure entrepreneurship not only addresses concerns about innovative components, inclusiveness of incorporated self-employment, but also avoids some of the problems associated with other measures that are typically used in the literature. Elderly entrepreneurs as measured in the empirical study of this book include two groups of seniors: those seniors who establish new businesses after the age of 62, and entrepreneurs who continue to be entrepreneurs after the age of 62.

7.1 Age and Occupational Choices

Descriptive statistics were generated using the U.S. Census 2000 *Public Use Microdata Samples* (PUMS) 1-percent sample data[33]. Some of the advantages of this data include that it has detailed information broken down by age going all the ways up to age 90, the information can be extracted for different geographic units—State, County, Public Use Microdata Sample Areas (PUMAs), Metropolitan Statistical Areas (MSAs), Primary Metropolitan Statistical Areas (PMSAs), and Consolidated Metropolitan Statistical Areas (CMSAs)[34], it contains detailed socio-economic information, and it has a large sample size. The PUMS sample contains over 2.8 million individuals, 1.66 million employed people and 0.44 million seniors. The data it offers is much more detailed and information-rich than some of the other large-scale datasets that have been used for the study of seniors, such as Health and Retirement Study (HRS).

While the PUMS 1-percent sample offers a large quantity of observations. It should be noted that the estimates derived from the U.S. Census sample files are expected to differ from the 100-percent figures because they are subject to sampling and non-sampling errors. Each

---

[33] Instead of PUMS 5-percent samples and previously used Health and Retirement Study (HRS) data. HRS only offers age information till 57 and PUMS 5-percent does not offer as flexible geographic identification information.

[34] The flexible geographic identification (state and metro area) of PUMS 1-percent samples makes it more possible to integrate data from other sources.

observation in the PUMS database contains a weight that can be used to estimate the frequency of a particular characteristic in the entire population.

The descriptive statistics reveal that a higher proportion of younger workers than the older ones are unpaid family workers and the self-employment rate among seniors is higher than that among the young. There is a similar rate among the two groups for private sector employment, government employment, and unemployment. This is illustrated in Figures 7.1 and 7.2. Seventy-five percent of younger workers are unpaid family workers, while only 63% of older workers are under the same category. The higher share for unpaid family workers among younger people in the labor force might be largely contributed by housewives who staying home taking care of children, while most seniors are relieved from responsibilities for children. Many seniors, though, have the obligations to take care other family members who are older or sick or their grandchildren. Nineteen percent of the elderly (62+) in the labor force are self-employed, as compared to 9% for their younger cohort (16- 61)[35] in 2000. The self-employment rate among seniors who are in the labor force is more than twice as much as that of the younger group. This indicates seniors' strong occupational preference for self-employment. For every five seniors who are in the labor force, about one of them is self-employed. This high self-employment rate among older workers is worth further attention.

---

[35] though the older cohort has a higher proportion of people who are not employed or not in the labor force.

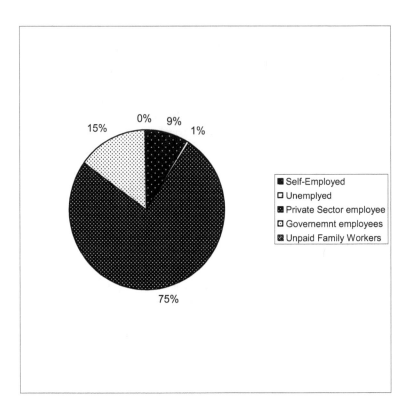

Figure 7.1 Percentages of Younger Workers by Employment Type in 2000
Source: Zhang (2008).

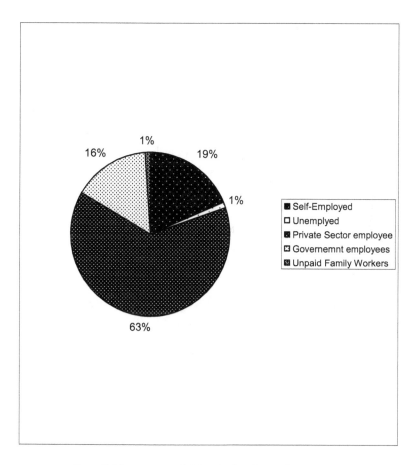

Figure 7.2 Percentages of Older Workers by Employment Type in 2000
Source: Zhang (2008).

However, when examining self-employment rates relative to the entire population rather than just the labor force, seniors' self-employment rate is only slightly lower than the rate associated with the young. The details of the data to support this finding are given in Appendix 7.1, cited from Zhang (2008). The labor force participation rate for seniors is much lower than that of the younger cohorts; this is perhaps due to differences between the two age groups in health, family responsibilities, and life goals. The lower labor force participation rate among seniors helps to explain why seniors have a lower self-employment rate in the entire population but a higher self-employment rate in the labor force than the young.

Older people who participate in the labor force tend to have a higher self-employment rate than the younger ones and that the self-employment rates generally increase with age except for oldest age cohorts (starting from late 80s). Figure 7.3 displays the self-employment rates in the population as a whole, in the labor force, and in the employed population. The raw data for this figure is provided in Appendix 7.2 and 8.3[36]. The top two curves of this figure show that self-employment rates in the labor force and in employment both increase with age since the age of 20, though there is some fluctuation in this trend for the oldest cohorts (over 88). The bottom curve, which shows the proportion of self-employment in the population, displays a nearly normal distribution with peak around the ages 52 to 62. The discrepancies between self-employment rates in the labor force and self-employment rates in the population reveal that many seniors do not participate in the labor force. Once they participate in the labor force, they are more likely to be self-employed than the younger workers.

---

[36] Appendix 7.2 presents the counts of people for each variable, while Appendix 7.4, 7.5, 7.6 presents the rates or percentages in Figure 7.3, 7.4, and 7.5 respectively.

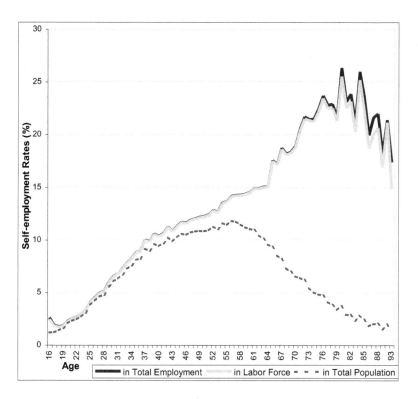

Figure 7.3 Self-employment Rates by Age

Source: Zhang (2008).

The rates associated with wage and salary employment look much different from those associated with self-employment, particularly when comparing seniors to younger individuals. In fact, the pattern of wage and salary employment rates in the labor force is nearly opposite to that of self-employment rates. Figure 7.4 shows that the wage-and-salary employment rate in the labor force (shown as the top curve) begins to decrease around the age of 20 or so. The raw data for this figure is presented in Appendix 7.2 and 7.5. In conclusion, seniors have higher self-employment rates, but lower wage-and-salary employment rates than the younger employed individuals. Therefore the following sections of this chapter focus on seniors' self-employment.

It also appears that seniors over 70 have higher unemployment[37] rates than the younger cohorts. Figure 7.4 shows that the unemployment rate in labor force (indicated by the bottom dashed curve) begins to increase around the age of 70. This possibly partially relates to age discrimination.

---

[37] Unemployment is part of the labor force, like various employments.

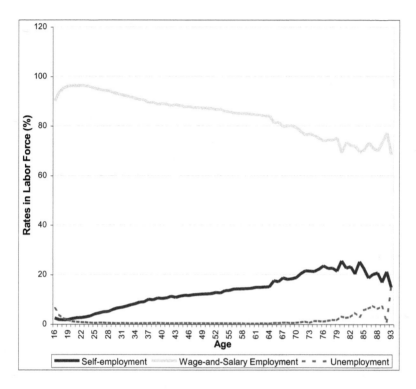

Figure 7.4 Self-employment Rates vs. Wage-and-salary Employment Rates in the Labor Force by Age
Source: Zhang (2008).

7.2 Elderly Self-employment in the "Knowledge Economy"

As indicated earlier, the "Knowledge Economy" offers more opportunities to the elderly than the "Fordist economy". In the "Knowledge Economy", knowledge and human capital, which are characterized by such factors as experience, information, skills, education attainment, social network, and health (Becker, 1986, 1992, 1990, 1993), have become a central element for

113

economic growth in the "Knowledge Economy". Seniors possess many of these above human capital factors through their cumulative working experience. Seniors tend to possess a higher level of management skills, mentoring, a mature social network, and job-specific skills. The types of jobs that define the "Knowledge Economy" also tend to be less physically and location demanding than the manufacturing based "Fordist economy". The smaller physical and location limitations make it more possible for elders to be more involved in the labor force. The "footloose" characteristic, i.e. the location freedom, facilitated by information technology reduces the limitation of older people's mobility, which further enhances older people's human capital in the "Knowledge Economy". As indicated previously, this book defines the "Knowledge Economy" through creative class occupations. *Creative class*, as introduced earlier, is a concept Florida (2004) uses to describe the characteristics of our current economy and is explained as a key indicator of growth.

Of those seniors who are self-employed, a majority is in the knowledge-based occupations (or creative class); this is in contrast to the young, who as a whole are primarily employed in non-knowledge-based sectors. This finding is illustrated in Figure 7.5 and 7.6 (see data table in Appendix 7.5).

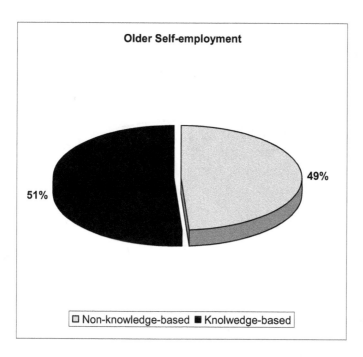

Figure 7.5 Proportion of Knowledge-based vs. Non-knowledge-based Self-employment among Seniors in 2000[38]
Source: Zhang (2008).

---

[38] Data table for this figure presentation is displayed in Appendix 7.5.

Figure 7.6 Proportion of Knowledge-based vs. Non-knowledge-based Self-employment among Younger Cohorts in 2000[39]
Source: Zhang (2008).

Seniors also have higher self-employment rates than the young for each of the major occupational sectors that fall under the classification of knowledge-based sectors (or the categories of creative class) and for non-knowledge-based sectors as a whole. This is illustrated in Figure 7.7, which compares side-by-side the self-employment rates of seniors and younger individuals in the labor force by occupational category. The self-employment rates associated

---

[39] Data table for this figure presentation is displayed in Appendix 7.5.

with seniors more than double that of younger individuals for all of the knowledge-based (or creative class occupations), except the sector *Arts & Entertainment* [Standard Occupational Classification code (SOC) = 27].

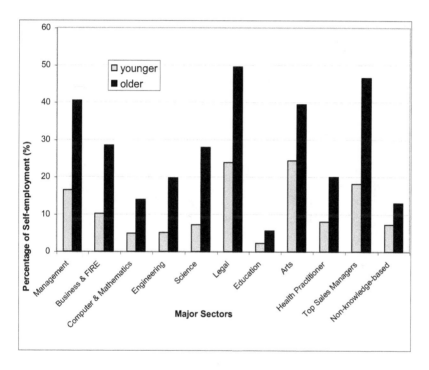

Figure 7.7 Self-employment Rate by Major Sectors, Older vs. Younger Workers in 2000
Source: Zhang (2008).

The distribution of self-employed seniors across the knowledge-based occupations and non-knowledge-based professions as a whole highlights a slightly different pattern in relation to the respective distribution for the young. Figure 7.8 shows the percentage breakdown by occupational class for seniors and the younger labor force participants. When viewed in this manner, seniors' self-employment is more specialized in the knowledge-based occupations, compared to that of the younger cohorts. The exceptions are the two sectors—*Computer & Mathematics* (SOC=15) and *Arts & Entertainment* (SOC=27). Both groups show similar concentration in *Legal, Education,* and *Health Practitioner* occupations, but seniors' self-employment is evidently more concentrated than their younger counterparts in most knowledge sectors—*Management, Business & Finance, Architecture & Engineering, Physical & Social science,* and High-level Sales Management. Younger entrepreneurs accordingly tend to concentrate more than seniors in the non-knowledge-based economy.

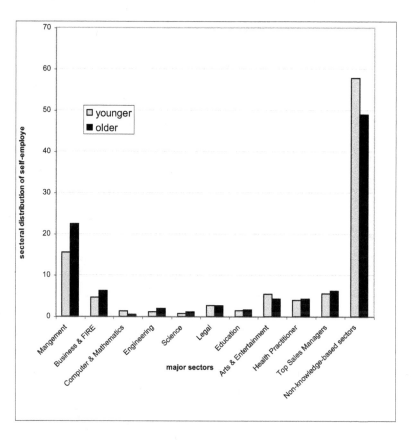

Figure 7.8 Sectoral Distribution of Older vs. Younger Self-employed in 2000
Source: Zhang (2008).

7.3 Age and Entrepreneurship in the "Knowledge Economy"

Seniors in the labor force have a higher self-employment rate than the younger group and seniors self-employment, as compared to their younger counterparts, tend to concentrate in knowledge-based sectors. This situation evidences the elderly friendliness of the "Knowledge Economy".

As this book addresses situations in the "Knowledge Economy", the following of the chapter then focuses on self-employment only in the knowledge-based sectors, i.e., entrepreneurship. Considering the innovation and knowledge components in the nature of entrepreneurship, entrepreneurship is defined in this book as knowledge-based self-employment instead of self-employment in all economic sectors. The previous section presented through descriptive statistics both self-employment rates and knowledge-based self-employment rates among seniors versus among the younger cohorts. It is obvious that, compared to the younger working cohorts, seniors not only have a higher self-employment rate in the labor force, but also have a much higher knowledge-based self-employment rate. Based on those data, seniors are expected more likely to be entrepreneurs than younger working people. To test this hypothesis, a binomial logit model is estimated in Zhang (2007a) to more rigorously explore how someone's age influences their propensity to be an entrepreneur, controlling for certain other characteristics of the individual.

This binomial logit model was based on the utility maximization theory introduced in Zhang (2008). The model was estimated using the 1-percent sample of individuals from the 2000 PUMS database. The dependent variable in the model is the probability that an individual is an entrepreneur, given their age, other demographic variables, and socio-economic characteristics. Age is specified in the model as a dummy variable, where "1" indicates a senior (age 62 or over) and "0" for younger people of working ages (age 16-61). The model controls for a number of characteristics specific to the individuals that are consistent with other models that have been developed in previous literature to examine seniors' occupational choices. Those control factors affecting seniors' entrepreneurial propensity include health conditions (Quinn, 1980), educational levels (Berkovec and Stern, 1991), wealth (Bruce et. al., 2000; Parker and Rougaier, 2004), and other demographic characteristics (such as race, gender, marriage status, and citizenship). The statistical details of this model estimation and the details of the variable

120

measurement and descriptions are explained in Zhang (2007a). The specification of the binomial model is:

$$\ln[P_i/(1- P_i)] = \alpha_0 + \phi \text{Age}_i + \Sigma\beta_m \text{X}_m,$$

or

$$P(Y_i =1 \mid \text{Age}, \text{X}_m) = \frac{1}{1+\exp (-\alpha_0 - \phi \text{Age}_i - \sum \beta_m X_m)} \quad , \tag{7.1}$$

where

$P(Y=1, Age, X_m)$ is the probability that an individual i is an entrepreneur given their age, other demographic and socio-economic characteristics;

Y_i is a binary variable with value "1" indicating the status of an entrepreneur and "0" indicating the status of a wage-and-salary employee;

Age_i is a binary variable with value "1" referring to individuals of age 62 or greater and "0" referring to those under 62 and of working age (16-61);

$\Sigma\beta_m X_m$ measures m other factors that are related to the individuals. Those factors have been identified in the literature to influence the probability that an individual will be an entrepreneur. Those factors include income, property value, educational level, disability status, gender, marital status, citizenship, and race. Among them, disability status is used as a proxy for health conditions. Appendix 7.6 displays all of the variables in the model and their sources of data.

The estimated results of the above model offer some interesting findings. The results indicate that there is a statistically significant (p=0.0000) and positive relationship between being a senior and being an entrepreneur, controlling for other demographic and socioeconomic characteristics of the person. More specifically, seniors are more likely than younger individuals to be entrepreneurs. The coefficient on *being a senior* is 0.83 (shown in Appendix 7.7). This means that the log of the odds of someone being an entrepreneur increases by 0.83 if they are aged 62 or over (rather than within the age range of 16-61), controlling for other characteristics of the individual. In fact, this variable has the strongest impact on entrepreneurial propensity out of all of the dummy variables in the model.

All of the other characteristics of an individual that are specified in the model were found to be important determinants of entrepreneurship. Human capital is found to associate with entrepreneurial propensity. One human capital indicator, education attainment, has a positive effect on the likelihood of being an entrepreneur. Additional levels of education an individual has achieved enhance the log of the odds for this person to participate in the labor force as entrepreneurs. Another human capital indicator, health condition, is also found to relate to entrepreneurial propensity. This chapter uses employment disability status as a proxy for health conditions. Individuals with employment disabilities were found to be more likely to be entrepreneurs, a finding which on the face may appear to be somewhat counterintuitive. Individuals with disabilities face barriers to entry into wage-and-salary employment due to discriminatory attitudes on the part of employers, and consequently, self-employment may be a more attractive option for them. Disability may face discrimination in wage-and-salary workplace, which could increase an individual's chance to choose entrepreneurship as an outlet of a career. Further, a person's employment disability may make them more strong-willed and independent, which allows them to excel in an entrepreneurial setting.

Gender, the immigration status, marital circumstances, and race of an individual were also found to be important determinants of entrepreneurship. Being a male has a strong association with an individual's chance to be an entrepreneur. Newer immigrants are more likely to be entrepreneurs[40], but the impact of this factor is relatively small[41]. In comparison to those who are separated, the widowed, the divorced, and the married are more likely to be entrepreneurs and singles less likely. Of all of these categories, being single appears to matter

---

[40] The variable *Year to U.S.* is measured by the year an individual came to the United States. For a newly immigrated person, the value of this variable (e.g. 2000, 1999, 1998, etc.) is larger.

[41] The impact of immigration factor is 0.000055 according to Appendix 7.7 and Zhang (2007a).

the most. The coefficient on this dummy variable, while negative, is much larger than those that are associated with the other marriage status categories. Being white, Asian or being of mixed descent, compared to people of other races, increases one's odds of being an entrepreneur. On the other hand, those who are Black are less likely to be entrepreneurial.

Those with money are more likely to be entrepreneurs. The coefficients on both of the wealth indicators, i.e., household income and property value, are significant (p=0.0000) and positive. The coefficient on property value is big[42], but the coefficient on household income is small[43]. This situation indicates that property value has a strong association with an individual's entrepreneurial propensity while a person's household income has a weak effect, controlling for other factors. Wealth and income provides an individual with the financial capital that is often necessary to start a business and so it is not surprising to find out that those with more assets are more likely to be entrepreneurial.

The responsibility of taking care of grandchildren has a negative impact on the likelihood that someone is an entrepreneur and this is largely a function of the duration of care taking. More specifically, the longer a person has had the responsibilities of taking care of grandchildren, the less likely they are to be entrepreneurs. Taking care of grandchildren for a longer period normally means detaching from the labor force and foregoing the development of new work-related skills and network building, which makes it eventually more difficult for them to start a business.

7.4 Conclusions

This chapter suggests that there is a correlation between age and occupational choices. Seniors' occupational preference is entrepreneurship. Older individuals have a higher self-employment rate than their younger cohorts and have a lower wage-and-salary employment rates

---

[42] The coefficient on property value is 0.046 according to Appendix 7.7 and Zhang (2007a).

[43] The coefficient on household income is 0.0000025 according to Appendix 7.7 and Zhang (2007a).

than the younger employed individuals. Seniors' self-employment tends to concentrate in the knowledge-based sectors. Compared with younger self-employment, elderly self-employment tends to concentrate in knowledge-based sectors, with the exception of those occupations in the sectors of Computer & Mathematics and Arts & Entertainment. This finding, though different, somewhat echoes senior workers' concentration and specialization in knowledge associated sectors that were preliminarily identified in Chapter 7.

A binomial logit model shows that seniors in the labor force are more likely to be entrepreneurs than the young. To be more specific, being of age 62 or over is associated with a higher propensity for entrepreneurship, controlling for other demographic and socioeconomic characteristics of individuals. The old-age factor in fact has a stronger impact than all other dummy variables in the model. All of the other characteristics of an individual that are specified in the model were found to be important determinants of entrepreneurial propensity. Individuals with higher education attainment, with employment disabilities, being male, of the race of White and Asian, having the responsibility for grandchildren for a shorter period of time, and owning a higher property value are found more likely to be an entrepreneur.

Part V Dynamics between Aging and the "Knowledge Economy": Empirics & Case Study

Chapter 8 the "Knowledge Economy" and Elderly Entrepreneurship

The previous part has shown that seniors are more likely to be self-employed and their self-employment tends to concentrate in the knowledge-based sectors. Seniors are more likely to be entrepreneurs. Seniors' unique occupation choice toward entrepreneurship makes it an interesting question whether this occupational preference, i.e., elderly entrepreneurship, is related to the "Knowledge Economy" and whether elderly entrepreneurship, as the book wished, spurs the growth of the "Knowledge Economy", mitigates aging related crises, and creates new opportunities.

Driven by knowledge, innovation, and entrepreneurship, the "Knowledge Economy" provides an unprecedented elderly-friendly environment to fertilize seniors' labor force participation, particularly in the knowledge-based sectors and for their entrepreneurship. The less physically demanding "Knowledge Economy" is built and grow on skills, experience, and social network. Seniors possess unique advantage of those assets. As introduced earlier, older people have a series of virtues contributing to their special human capital that younger people may not possess, such as interpersonal skills, rich working experience, mature social business network, and strong work ethic. All these virtues can increase the knowledge stock. The cumulated knowledge stock in the "Knowledge Economy" can eventually benefit seniors for their economic activities, as well as entrepreneurship.

. The large and growing retiree cohort is argued to drain the Social Security fund and result in a labor shortage (Peterson, 1999). With an increasingly large retirement population and a shrinking share for working population, each working-age person will have to support more and more retirees to meet the social demands, under the same or very similar technological and policy conditions (i.e., with the average retirement age staying at 62). This situation would not just mean an increasingly large demand for working people to support, but also a rising threat for an unreliable retirement life. The baby boomer generation makes this situation even worse.

This threat from an increasingly large retiree population includes a rising demand for the Social Security fund pay benefits. With a shrinking share of working people in the population but a rising demand for the Social Security fund pay benefits, the Social Security fund contribution that is based on payroll tax also relatively declines. This relatively declining Social Security fund contribution would eventually not be able to meet the increasing demand of the Social Security fund pay benefits and the Social Security system would face bankruptcy.

In this situation, whether elderly entrepreneurship can spur economic growth, help to mitigate the potential Social Security crisis and labor shortage becomes a fundamental and important research question. This chapter therefore empirically explores the economic, labor, and fiscal role of elderly entrepreneurship in the "Knowledge Economy".

8.1 The Hypotheses on the Economic Role of Elderly Entrepreneurship

As suggested in Part II of this book, entrepreneurship has been argued to be one of the major factors, like physical capital and labor, to drive regional economic growth (Audretsch and Keilbach, 2004), but whether elderly entrepreneurship is a significant factor, like entrepreneurship in general, that drives regional economy to grow is unknown. Considering the fact that seniors' pursuits differ from their younger counterparts, the economic role of elderly entrepreneurship could differ from that of the young. Many people believe that seniors are not as motivated as the young to try new creations and new methods and that seniors tend to stay with what they have been familiar with for many decades. If it were the case, elderly venture creation might not really generate much Schumpeter's "creative disruption" (1950) that leads to economic growth. If this assumption and argument were correct, elderly entrepreneurship would not be expected to generate as much positive impacts as younger entrepreneurship or entrepreneurship in general on economic growth.

However, there exists counter-argument. In the "Knowledge Economy", seniors have cumulated job skills, many years' working experience, established business ties, etc. All these contribute to knowledge capital that is a key drive for the growth of the "Knowledge Economy". Those special knowledge capital components make seniors very valuable in the "Knowledge

Economy". Chapter 7 has evidenced that elderly self-employment tends to concentrate in knowledge-based sectors, compared to younger people's self-employment. This situation evidences the argument that the "Knowledge Economy" offers a cultivating setting for seniors' entrepreneurship. In this case, it is expected in this book that elderly entrepreneurship have a positive impact on regional economic growth.

Although growth theories have been popular in general economic literature, it is not until recent decades that the economic role of entrepreneurship begins to be recognized and emphasized. Neoclassic economic theories recognized labor and physical capital as the two key factors driving economic growth. This set of theories seems to interpret well industrial economy (or Fordist economy) and even agricultural economy, but it leaves a big "Solow residual" unexplained in empirical studies. Also, this set of theories, though with several attempts, does not explain well technological shifts. Technological conditions are set to be given in this set of theories.

When the Fordist economy began to transfer to the "Knowledge Economy", economists observe the rising importance of knowledge, information, and innovation. Cultivated and also pushed by the information technology, the role of knowledge, information, and human capital began to be formally integrated in the growth model. Here comes the new growth theory which adds a non-rival (or partially rival) quasi public good, knowledge capital, to physical capital and labor as key economic growth drivers. This new element, compared with the traditional two factors, labor and physical capital, has a special property—non-diminishing returns to scale. Therefore, knowledge capital not only explains economic growth, but also helps to explain why the economy could keep growing. Technological conditions are integrated inside the new growth theory models as a changing factor that drives economic growth. Therefore, the new growth theories are also called endogenous growth theories.

Yet, new growth theories are not the end of the story. In addition to lacking a mature widely accepted model for this set of theories, new growth theories still do not explain well where knowledge comes from. Not all knowledge is usable. There exists a knowledge filtering effect. In this case, location theories join the growth theories to explain the distance decaying effect of knowledge. Regional economic growth thus catches more academic attention. Entrepreneurship, though it has been popular in mostly microeconomic and organization theories, has eventually been observed to join knowledge capital to become a factor for economic growth. The special role of entrepreneurship in regional economic growth can be partially explained by its knowledge filtering effect. Entrepreneurship, through its innovation or "creative destruction", either creates something new by applying and spreading new knowledge or reallocates resources by promoting knowledge spillovers.

If entrepreneurship in general can be an important factor that contributes to the economic growth, how about elderly entrepreneurship? Does elderly entrepreneurship contribute to the regional economic growth as well? If so, does the contribution from elderly entrepreneurship is as large as that from entrepreneurship in general, or even larger? Chapter 6 has shown that the elderly are more likely to be self-employed and seniors' self-employment tends to concentrate in knowledge-based sectors. Seniors are also more likely to be entrepreneurs, as Zhang (2008) indicate. In the meantime, the "Knowledge Economy", as mentioned previously in this chapter, possibly offers a better socioeconomic environment for the elderly to participate in economic activities. In this case, if entrepreneurship in general contributes to economic growth, elderly entrepreneurship is expected to generate positive externalities to the economic growth as well.

It is in this special social background—an aging population and the "Knowledge Economy"—that elderly entrepreneurship becomes particularly meaningful and is expected to generate special positive contribution to economic growth. This chapter focuses on the economic contribution of elderly entrepreneurship at the metropolitan area level and addresses whether elderly entrepreneurship has a positive impact on economic growth across a heterogeneous set of metropolitan areas. It extends the Solow growth model formulated by Audretsch and Keilbach (2004) to test two hypotheses. First, elderly entrepreneurship is expected to have a positive and important role in fostering regional economic growth. Second, elderly entrepreneurship is hypothesized to have even a stronger impact on regional economic growth than entrepreneurship from younger working age people.

8.2 The Economic Growth Model

To examine the impact from the elderly self-employment on regional economic growth, Zhang (2008) extended the Audretsch and Keilbach (2004) but based on Solow's (1957) growth model

$$Y = A(t)K^{\beta}L^{1-\beta} \qquad (8.1)$$

Where, Y is output, K represents physical capital, L is labor, and $A(t)$ technical change through time t.

The extended base economic model:

$$Y_i/L = \alpha^{\beta 0}(K_i/L)^{\beta 1}R_i^{\beta 3}E_i^{\beta 4}e_i^{\varepsilon}, \text{ where } \beta_1 + \beta_2 = 1. \qquad (8.2)$$

where R_i represents the knowledge capital of region i, E_i represents entrepreneurship capital in the region, α represents the constant, and all of the other variables follow from the basic Solow model. Audretsch and Keilbach (2004) measure the economic growth of a region (Yi) by its Gross Value Added, corrected for the purchases of goods and services, VAT, and shipping costs. Physical capital (Ki) in their model is characterized by capital stock in the manufacturing and labor (Li) by total employment. Knowledge capital (Ri) is defined by the number of public and private sector employees engaged in research and development. The number of start-ups relative to population is used to measure entrepreneurship (Ei).

The corresponding regression model is:

$$\log(Y_i/L) = \beta_0 \log\alpha + \beta_1 \log(K_i/L) + \beta_3 \log Ri + \beta_4 \log E_i + v_i, \qquad (8.3)$$

130

This model assumes that the total of coefficients for capital and labor is set to be 1. To be more specific, this model assumes constant returns to scale for capital stock and labor and constant elasticity of substitution.

The above per labor entrepreneurship growth model is used to explore the role of entrepreneurship in the regional economic growth. To incorporate elderly entrepreneurship and consider the spatial effect, a *sensitivity analysis* and a *spatial analysis* were also performed in Zhang (2008).

After running spatial diagnostics tests, either spatial lag or spatial error model will be selected. For example, assuming spatial lag models will be more appropriate than spatial error models, the final model results in the following:

$$\log(Y/L) = \rho W_{\log(Y/L)} + \beta 0 \log \alpha + \beta 1 * \log(K/L) + \beta 3 * \log R + \beta 4 * \log E + v_i, \quad (8.4)$$

$$\log(Y/L) = \rho W_{\log(Y/L)} + \beta 0' \log \alpha' + \beta 1' * \log(K/L) + \beta 3' * \log R + \beta 4' * \log(\text{elderly } E) + v_i', \quad (8.5)$$

$$\log(Y/L) = \rho W_{\log(Y/L)} + \beta 0'' \log \alpha'' + \beta 1'' * \log(K/L) + \beta 3'' * \log R + \beta 4'' * \log(\text{elderly } E) + \beta 5'' * \log(\text{younger } E) + v_i'' \cdot \quad (8.6)$$

where $\rho W_{\log(Y/L)}$ captures the spatially lagged effects.

8.3 Empirical Evidence of Elderly Entrepreneurship's Economic Role

Zhang (2008) used Primary Metropolitan Statistic Areas (PMSAs) or Metropolitan Statistics Areas (MSAs) as the geographic unit of analysis and empirically estimated the above spatial per labor models with sensitivity analysis. The reasons for selecting PMSAs and MSAs as units of analysis for this study, in addition to data availability, include: First, the PMSA / MSA offers a certain level of homogeneity in employment and commuting patterns; the economic characteristics inside this geographic scale are much more homogeneous than those at the state level (Glaeser et al., 1995). Second, cities are the significant source of innovation due to the great diversity of knowledge (Jacob, 1969). Third, the unit has been often used in many other sub-national studies on regional development. Other sub-national units, states, counties or Combined Metropolitan Statistical Areas (CMSAs), are not as appropriate as PMSAs and MSAs.

The data sources used in the Zhang (2008) study is Public Use Micro Samples (PUMS) 2000 data, the Bureau of Economic Analysis 2000 data, and the American Community Survey 2005 data. Appendix 8.2 describes the variables. The details on how to extract data and use them to measure the variables in the above models are introduced in Zhang (2007c). To make it brief, the **physical capital** variable (K) is measured through the per labor value of fixed assets (private and public sectors) at the PMSA / MSA level[44]. The **labor** variable (L) is measured by the total employment at the PMSA / MSA level, including wage and salary employees and the self-employed. In the per labor entrepreneurship model, the labor variable is divided by the **capital stock variable** (K) across PMSAs / MSAs.

The **entrepreneurship capital** variable (E) is measured by the percentage of incorporated and unincorporated self-employers who belong to the knowledge-based sectors relative to the total population at the PMSA / MSA level[45]. The **knowledge capital** variable (R)

---

[44] This process follows Garofalo and Yamarik (2002). Details of this process are introduced in Zhang (2007c).

[45] Although Audretsch and Keilbach (2004) use the number of new start-ups to measure entrepreneurship, data on start-ups by the age of business owners was not available. Self-employment has been mentioned as the best-available measurement of senior entrepreneurship (Evans and Leighton 1989, Blanchflower et al. 2001); this revised definition that uses seniors' self-employment in knowledge-based sector would be even better and closer to the knowledge concept of entrepreneurship, compared to the measure that uses self-employment in general. One concern in using self-employment data as a measure of entrepreneurship is that, while knowledge base and innovation are the key components that make the concept of entrepreneurship appealing, self-employed businesses are not necessarily innovative and many are low-tech personal or family-owned businesses that fall into the class of self-employed businesses. To address this, only knowledge-based self-employment is considered in the measure of entrepreneurship. Creative class, although focused more on creativity rather than innovation and knowledge, is a decent proxy for knowledge-based occupations. Knowledge-based self-employment or analytic self-employer class is used specifically to characterize entrepreneurship. Another problem of using self-employment as a measure for entrepreneurship is that, in many cases, self-employment is characterized as a sole

132

is measured by the number of people who have attained postgraduate education. Although Bachelor's degree holders are often used as a measure for knowledge capital, it is believed here that postgraduate education has a stronger impact on R&D than Bachelor's level education attainment. The **output** variable (Y) is measured by the median personal income of a PMSA / MSA.

The estimation results in Zhang (2008) confirm that a spatial lag model is an appropriate formulation for Models (8.4), (8.5), and (8.6) and the spatial dependence factor, the spatial lags for each model, were found to be highly significant (all $ps<=0.01$, as shown in Table 8.1). This indicates that the regional growth in a MSA / PMSA is influenced by the regional growth of the first-order nearest metropolitan areas (i.e., MSAs and PMSAs), according to the distance threshold, controlling for the other variables in the model.

---

proprietorship or partnership and incorporated business owners are typically not included. To avoid this problem, the data used for self-employment includes incorporated self-employment as well as unincorporated self-employment. In addition, measuring entrepreneurship by self-employment avoids problems of two other commonly used measures. The use of R&D expenditures tends to underestimate small-business entrepreneurship (Acs and Audretsch 1990) and the measure by startups (Audretsch and Keilbach 2004) does not necessarily capture the innovation component of entrepreneurship either. The model considers only the static value of PMSA / MSA knowledge-based self-employment rate (or quantity), which may not accurately characterize establishment of the new startups by the elderly. However, data on elderly (aged 62 and above) startups was not available. Using the regional growth rate of elderly knowledge-based self-employment was once considered to be an avenue for measuring the establishment of new businesses by the elderly; but regional growth in elderly knowledge-based self-employment does not necessarily reflect the actual levels of elderly startups. Business death and migration contribute partially to the change of self-employment levels45. Therefore, the model uses a cross-sectional static measure of entrepreneurship. This static measure is consistent with the notion of the production-function-based growth model

Table 8.1 Regression results and diagnostic tests for Spatial Lag Model

Dependent variable: Economic output—2005 Median personal income		Spatial Lag Models parameters		
Independent variables		Model (9.4)	Model (9.5)	Model (9.6)
K	Per labor capital	0.2043691***	0.1036223**	0.1034293**
		(4.16)	(2.5)	(2.5)
R (#)	# Attained postgraduate education	0.0517804***	0.0666594***	0.0677358***
		(3.62)	(5.58)	(5.35)
E (%)	% Entrepreneur among population	0.1111273***		
		(2.62)		
	% Elderly Entrepreneur among elderly		0.1263556***	0.1293551***
			(3.7)	(3.58)
	% Young Entrepreneur among young working people			-0.0138458
				(-0.26)
	Rho	0.4036052***	0.3590498***	0.3563363***
		(3.16)	(2.79)	(2.76)
	Constant	3.474251**	5.003107***	4.983334***
		(2.54)	(3.53)	(3.51)
Observations		90	90	90
Log likelihood		**77.154915**	**80.260636**	**80.293583**
Variance ratio		0.444	0.486	0.487
Squared corr.		0.484	0.514	0.514
Sigma		0.10	0.10	0.10
Wald test of rho=0: chi2(1) =		**9.991 [0.002]**	**7.788 [0.005]**	**7.609 [0.006]**
Likelihood ratio test of rho=0:chi2(1) =		**8.452 [0.004]**	**6.831 [0.009]**	**6.679 [0.010]**
Lagrange multiplier test of rho=0: chi2(1) =		**9.760 [0.002]**	**7.930 [0.005]**	**7.686 [0.006]**
Acceptable range for rho:		-1.169 < rho < 1.000		
Weight matrix type		Distance-based (inverse distance, row		

	standardized)
Distance band	0.0 < d <= 5.5

Elderly entrepreneurship is found to have a significant [p=0.000 in Model (9.5) and (9.6)] and positive impact on regional growth. Younger entrepreneurship, on the other hand, is now found to be insignificant [p=0.797 in Model (10.6)] and the effects of this factor on regional growth are negative. It should be noted that entrepreneurship for all age groups as a whole is significant [p=0.009 in Model (10.4)]. The estimation results along with the levels of significance for each of the coefficients are presented in Table 8.1.

For every 1% increase in the proportion of elderly entrepreneurs in any given MSA / PMSA elderly population, there is a corresponding 0.13% increase in median personal income for that area, ceteris paribus. This impact is lagged by five years. The technical details on why a five-year lag is selected are explained in Zhang (2008). Compared with the other traditional factors that drive regional economic growth – i.e., physical capital and knowledge capital, elderly entrepreneurship was found to have a stronger impact. Ceteris paribus, each additional 1% increase in per capita physical capital generates a 0.10% increase in median personal income in a metropolitan area, while each additional 1% increase in postgraduate education attainment generates a 0.07% increase in metropolitan median personal income.

Elderly entrepreneurship is also found to have a stronger impact on regional economic growth than that associated with entrepreneurship across all age groups, and much stronger than that from younger entrepreneurs. Controlling for other factors, for every 1% increase in the proportion of all-age entrepreneurs in a given metropolitan population, there is a 0.11% increase in median personal income for that MSA / PMSA; the increase in the proportion of younger entrepreneurs in a given metropolitan younger population has an insignificant negative effect on the corresponding MSA / PMSA median income.

Based on the regression diagnostics, the log likelihood is strong, which helps to confirm that the spatial lag model is a better fit than the spatial error model. However, the residual map (see Appendix 8.1) after applying the spatial model still displays a substantial level of clustering. This situation indicates the presence of some regional spatial autocorrelation, as delineated in Zhang (2008). Therefore, there might still exist some model misspecification issues and future research to investigate the potential model misspecification issues would be worthy.

8.4 The Hypotheses on the Labor and Fiscal Role of Elderly Entrepreneurship

The potential labor shortage, the enlarging threat against guaranteed Social Security benefits, and growing social demands would result in an increasingly fierce competition for social resources and therefore a less and less reliable retirement life, if no major technological shift and policy enhancement were realized. After contributing heart and soul to social wealth for most of their life, seniors deserve a decent peaceful and reliable late life after they decide to withdraw from the labor force. Therefore, something needs to be done to mitigate the prognostic labor shortage and Social Security fund bankruptcy and to enhance seniors' late life.

Although various policy options have been proposed, they all have their own limitations, as previous chapters have indicated. In the meantime, involving more seniors in the labor force, particularly on a voluntary basis, is expected to largely help to balance the social resource supply and consumption demand. A possible approach to increase seniors' voluntary labor force participation is through entrepreneurship. Entrepreneurship could offer seniors more flexibility for their time and location arrangement, could provide them with more control of their own life, and could give them a large platform to make use of their own skills and fulfill their own ambitions. Many seniors, after years' working experience, have cumulated rich skill sets that not only provide expertise in certain aspects, but also build trustworthy social networks; many of them also have had management and executive experience. Given enough policy motivation, those seniors who want to continue their career ambitions and excitements or those seniors who need more financial supports would very possibly join the labor force as entrepreneurs.

136

Elderly entrepreneurs not just directly participate in the labor force and contribute to the payroll tax and Social Security fund contribution, but also help foster an economic environment that is more elderly friendly. This is particularly important for an aging society. Elderly entrepreneurs are possibly more likely to accept elderly employees than the younger entrepreneurs. For example, it is natural and easy for them to turn to their old colleagues/ bosses, long-term friends, and business partners who are mostly likely within the similar age ranges and share similar interests. Also, more active elderly entrepreneurs could help to improve social image of an active late life and indirectly motivate more seniors to join the labor force or to be more active in the society. Eventually, elderly entrepreneurship could help mitigate the potential labor shortage and Social Security crisis that is resulted from population aging under current technical and policy conditions.

Three hypotheses are then tested for elderly entrepreneurship's labor and fiscal role. First, it is hypothesized that a higher level of elderly entrepreneurship is associated with a larger labor force. Second, elderly entrepreneurship has a direct and positive association with the Social Security fund contribution. Third, through the jobs that elderly entrepreneurship creates and seniors' continued participation in the workforce, elderly entrepreneurs have an indirect and positive association with the Social Security fund contribution.

Elderly entrepreneurship is not just expected to create jobs, but also expected to expand the labor force size. Previous literature indicates that entrepreneurship and self-employment play a significant role in job creation (Picot and Manser, 1999; Acs and Armington, 2003; Van Stel and Storey, 2004; and Burker and Fitzroy, 2006). The same relationship is expected to hold for elderly entrepreneurship as well. Elderly entrepreneurship is hypothesized to contribute to enlarging the labor force size for three reasons. First, seniors' participation as entrepreneurs in the labor force contributes directly to the job pool. Second, entrepreneurial activities create wage-and-salary jobs in the economy (see Acs and Armington, 2003). Third, elderly entrepreneurs retire more gradually than elderly wage-and-salary employees (Quinn, 1980) and thus retain in the labor force for a longer period.

There are many reasons to believe that elderly entrepreneurship contributes positively to the Social Security fund. Since Social Security pay benefits are funded by taxes imposed on wages and salaries of employees and entrepreneurs, the size of the labor force directly contributes to the size of Social Security fund. Steuerle (2005) testified in the U.S. House of

Representatives that there is, in fact, a positive relationship between the labor force and the Social Security fund. Elderly entrepreneurship is hypothesized to have a positive impact on the Social Security fund through its contribution to the labor force. Elderly entrepreneurs are also expected to directly contribute to the Social Security fund, and this contribution would not be as much if they chose to participate in wage-and-salary jobs instead. Elderly entrepreneurs pay 100% of their Social Security taxes, while wage-and-salary employees pay only 50%.

8.5 The Model for Elderly Entrepreneurship's Labor and Fiscal Roles

A path analysis model is used in Zhang (2008) to verify and quantify the direct and indirect effects of senior entrepreneurship on the labor force and the Social Security fund. The conceptual specification of the path model captures the relationships between the variables that have been hypothesized to ultimately affect the Social Security fund. Figure 8.1 illustrates the model. Brackets between variables indicate the expected signs of the path coefficients in the model. To be more specific, elderly entrepreneurship is hypothesized in this model to affect wage-and-salary employment and then indirectly affect the labor force (or total employment[46]); eventually, through the impact on the total employment, elderly entrepreneurship affects the Social Security fund contribution. In the meantime, the direct impacts from elderly entrepreneurship on the total employment and the Social Security fund are also modeled. All the path coefficients are expected to be positive due to the logic that is introduced above.

---

[46] Labor force is the combination of total employment and the unemployed. To control for the regional economic factors that affect unemployment rates, only total employment is used to represent the labor force. Since unemployment only contributes a very small portion of the labor force, total employment can basically represent the labor force.

138

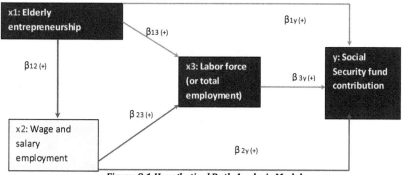

Figure 8.1 Hypothetical Path Analysis Model
Source: Zhang (2008)

The path model is based on several assumptions, as most path analysis models: (1) All relations in the model are linear and additive; (2) The residuals or error terms are uncorrelated with each other or with the variables in the model; (3) The causal flow is one-way; (4) The variables are measured without error for perfect reliability.

A Pearson's correlation coefficient matrix was first generated between each pair of variables that are hypothesized to have causal relationships in the model. To estimate and compare the direct and indirect effects between variables, standardized beta path coefficients (ranging from -1.0 to $+1.0$) were estimated using linear regressions. The details, including the spatial extensions, of this path analysis are explained in Zhang (2008).

Two datasets are used to estimate this path model: the U.S. Census 2000 *Public Use Microdata Samples* (PUMS) 1-percent sample data[47] and Social Security trust fund data for each state in the United States. All variables are of the value of year 2000. The units of analysis are states. The variables and their sources of data are summarized in Table 8.2. This test did not use

---

[47] Instead of PUMS 5-percent samples and previously used Health and Retirement Study (HRS) data. This dissertation consistently uses 1-percent PUMS samples data because of the flexible geographic identifiers. HRS data, although used heavily in previous aging related studies, is not used because of its limited age information beyond age 57.

Health and Retirement Study (HRS) data because HRS only offers age information till 57 or 59 for the latest data.

To avoid multicollinearity issues in regressions and also considering the different value scales of those variable, the variables are all measured in different formats to capture various forms of marginal change. The details on the measurement and description of the variables are presented in Zhang (2008). Table 8.2 summarizes the variable measurements and data sources. Appendix 8.3 describes all the variables used in this analysis.

Table 8.2 Summary of Variables

For path analysis model (state level)				
Variable	Description	Type	Sources	Scale
# of Elderly entrepreneurs	Number of elderly knowledge-based (or creative class) self-employment; recoded from variable occupation (SOC), "class of workers" and age in PUMS dataset.	Numerical	PUMS	State
Wage-and-salary employment share among Total Employment	Wage & salary employment/ total employment; recoded from variable "class of workers" in PUMS dataset.	Numerical	PUMS	State
Log (Employment)	Log (Total employment); recoded from variable "class of workers" in PUMS dataset.	Numerical	PUMS	State
Log (Social Security Contribution)	Log (Social Security contribution)	Numerical	SSA	State

8.6 Empirical Evidence on Elderly Entrepreneurship's Labor and Fiscal Role

A Pearson correlation coefficient matrix (see Appendix 8.4) provides information on the strength of linear relationship between pairs of variables in the path model.

Figure 8.2 presents the estimated path coefficients (standardized beta regression coefficients). The detailed regression analysis [including those of linear ordinary least square (OLS) regressions as well as those of spatial regression] are presented in Zhang (2008). Appendix 8.5 through 9.9 present the regression estimation results. Each of the regression model was first estimated using Ordinary Least Squares (OLS). Diagnostics test were performed to detect multicollinearity, heteroskedasticity, and spatial autocorrelation (through the global Moran's I test).

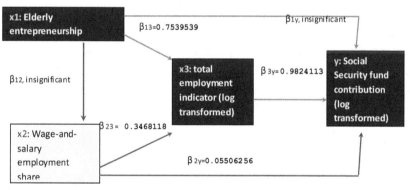

Figure 8.3 Path Analysis Model Estimation Results
Source: Zhang (2008).

All regressions estimate standardized coefficients and the path coefficients (shown in Figure 8.3) use the standardized coefficients of the best models.

The total effect (0.7540) is close to the correlation coefficient (0.7854) between elderly entrepreneurship and total employment[48]. This could indicate that this part of the model provides an acceptable or good fit and it helps to reemphasize that there is a strong relationship between elderly entrepreneurship and the size of total employment.

The total effect of elderly entrepreneurship on the Social Security fund contribution is 0.7407, also close to the correlation coefficient (0.7768). This could suggest that this path analysis model that tests the relationship between elderly entrepreneurship and the Social Security fund contribution also offers an acceptable fit.

However, the path through wage-and-salary employment does not seem to be viable for either the labor or Social Security effects. The direct effect from elderly entrepreneurship on the Social Security fund contribution is also insignificant. Further model specification might deserve to be explored to improve the model. Since path analysis is based on linear regressions and the Pearson correlation matrix is linear as well, there is possibility that a linear model transformed from some nonlinearity might make the model even better.

In general, the strong associations between elderly entrepreneurship and total employment and between elderly entrepreneurship and the Social Security fund contribution are evident. This can be seen either from the Pearson correlation coefficients, the total path analysis model effects (as described above), or the standardized regression coefficient [e.g. in the case of labor effect of elderly entrepreneurship, as tested in Zhang (2007d). Additionally, this path analysis model reveals the role of space in the function of labor and the Social Security fund contribution. This displays a regional economic spillover effect.

8.7 Conclusion

Elderly entrepreneurship has a statistically positive impact on economic growth. This impact is even stronger than other two factors that are traditionally considered to drive economic growth—physical capital and knowledge capital. Compared with other entrepreneurship, elderly

---

[48] Again, the size of total employment represents the labor force participation for this analysis.

entrepreneurship shows a stronger impact on economic growth than entrepreneurship as a whole and definitely stronger than entrepreneurship of younger people (which displays an insignificant and negative effect on economic growth).

The per-labor entrepreneurship spatial lag model with sensitivity analysis turns out to have a good model fit. It is superior to the original entrepreneurship growth model by Audretsch and Keilbach (2004) in that it avoids multicollinearity problem, spatial dependence and heterogeneity, that the measure of knowledge capital by postgraduate education attainment avoids the redundancy with the measure of labor, and that this model singles the elderly entrepreneurship out and compares it with other types of entrepreneurship.

Elderly entrepreneurship is also tested in the empirical evidence to have a strong association with a state's employment sizes and the Social Security fund contribution. The total labor effect and total Social Security fund effect of elderly entrepreneurship shown in this study are not close to be small, instead, they are as strong as 0.75 and 0.74 respectively. This situation indicates that provoking more elderly entrepreneurship and developing a bigger quantity of elderly entrepreneurs (or knowledge-based elderly self-employers and business owners) could relate to a large increase in employment size and a large increase in the Social Security fund contribution. Therefore, developing elderly entrepreneurship could greatly help mitigate the prognostic labor force shortage and Social Security fund exhaustion that is predicted to result from the aging population in the next decades. The regressions used in this path analysis model also identify spatial impacts. Geographic proximity is also a factor in the labor and Social Security effects of elderly entrepreneurship.

The limitations of the two empirical studies are explained in details in Zhang (2008). The study on elderly entrepreneurship's economic role still follows previous literature on using Cobb Douglas entrepreneurship growth model with both the assumption of constant elasticity of substitution between capital and labor and the assumption of constant return to scales for capital and labor combined (but increasing returns for the total of all inputs—capital, labor, knowledge, and entrepreneurship are allowed). Therefore, further research might explore alternative formulations of the model, like a translog production function, which relax such strong assumptions. The study on elderly entrepreneurship's labor and fiscal roles uses a simple path analysis model with limited variables and a not-large sample size. More sophisticated model, such as simulation models, would worth further exploration and investigation in future studies.

143

Chapter 9 "Knowledge Economy" for Seniors: A Case Study in Advanced Traveler Information Systems

The previous chapter addresses the economic, labor, and fiscal roles of seniors' economic activities, in specific, elderly entrepreneurship. This chapter focuses on addressing the "Knowledge Economy" as an environment for seniors' life. A key foundation of the "Knowledge Economy" is the information technology, as introduced in Part II of this book. Information technology, although traditionally considered to be the magic for the young, could also benefit seniors. This chapter uses a case study on an information technology system to address how the "Knowledge Economy" is a beneficial economy for seniors. The information technology system to be introduced in this chapter is called the "Advanced Traveler Information System" (ATIS).

America faces a fundamental demographic shift as the nation's population ages. Moreover, senior Americans will continue to demand the right to travel freely in personal automobiles. This demand makes seniors' mobility safety a crucial public policy issue. Traveler information systems, which help to manage the transportation network by informing drivers of current traffic conditions, will be increasingly important tools for managing traffic in situations where the aging population cohort is growing.

Traditional traveler information systems — radio or TV traffic reports — generally consider the needs of commuters and, therefore, might not serve senior travelers well. Thus, it is necessary to examine whether seniors have unique travel behavior and whether ATIS have a larger capacity than other traveler information systems, including broadcast traffic reports, to meet seniors' travel needs.

144

This chapter is structured as follows: Section 1 reviews literature on two topics separately -- ATIS and aging traveling population. Section 2 raises research questions and lists hypotheses. Section 3 explains the methodology this paper uses by defining some terms and generally reviewing how this paper analyzes and tests the hypotheses. The next section is for analysis and results. Section 5 discusses the limitations of ATIS in serving senior travelers. The last section presents conclusions of the analysis.

9.1 Traveler Information Systems

This section introduces traveler information systems and advanced traveler information system (ATIS). Previous literature on the ATIS is also summarized.

9.1.1 Current Traveler Information Systems and ATIS

A traveler information system is a valuable tool designed to manage transportation networks and to offer more options to travelers (Gilroy et al, 1998, p.8). The two primary modes of traveler information systems are called broadcasting and "narrowcasting" (Orski, n.d., p.3). The broadcasting system uses traditional radio and TV stations to offer frequent but "sketchy" traffic reports throughout a metro area during commuting hours (p.3). Orski uses the word "sketchy" to describe the simplicity of traveler information offered by radio and TV, suggesting that the information is limited and may fail to offer options, such as alternative routes. "Narrowcasting," in this context refers to ATIS – such as Smart Commuter, 511, and SmarTraveler -- which provide route-specific information via telephones or the Internet (p.3). Another traveler information system in addition to a broadcasting and a narrowcasting system is in-vehicle automated navigation systems, which offer en-route traveler information (Booz Allen and Hamilton, 1994).

Although broadcasting traveler information systems are still widely used, currently there is a growing variety of ATIS products and services available throughout the country (as shown in appendix 1). Using telephones or the Internet to transmit information, ATIS offers real-time traffic information available 24 hours a day and 7 days a week. For example, the Advanced

Regional Traffic Interactive Management and Information System (ARITMS) in the Kentucky and Ohio area updates reports about construction and traffic continuously between 6:00 a.m. and 7:00 p.m. Monday through Friday (Clemons et al, 1999). SmarTraveler, an ATIS, also updates its information as frequently as every five minutes (Toppen el al, 2002). Another ATIS, the 511 Traveler Information System in Nebraska is operated 24 hours a day and its information is made available by dialing 511 or accessing its website (Department of Transportation, 2002).

Along hwith frequent traveler information reports, ATIS is strongly supported by advanced technologies and various institutions: ATIS has widespread monitors with advanced technology to supervise the road condition; ATIS is sponsored by the state and local governments and private sectors. This type of support ensures ATIS the availability and accuracy of the following information: real-time camera viewing, prevailing speeds for highway segments, point-to-point route-specific traffic information, schedule and fare information, itinerary planning services, links to information about alternative modes of transportation and routes, and email addresses and telephone numbers for customer feedback (Soolman and Radin, 2000).

9.1.2 Acceptance of ATIS

Current literature documents the rising acceptance and advantages of ATIS, serving travelers of all age groups. The acceptance of ATIS is not only rising, but has also begun to show a stronger impact on people's life than the broadcasting traveler information systems which have been popular for decades.

The official website of the U.S. Department of Transportation, ITS (Intelligent Transportation Systems) Benefits and Costs Database, documents that ATIS has a greater effect on travelers' behavior than radio or TV broadcasts. Based on a survey in the San Francisco Bay area about the use of the TravInfo telephone and Internet traveler advisory service, the Department of Transportation report (2003) indicates that, after receiving ATIS route specific information, 81% of participants changed their travel plans for a safer and more efficient travel environment, whereas only 25% changed their travel plans after receiving information from radio and television broadcasts.

Reports about various ATIS products across the country have shown its rising popularity. For example, in the Kentucky and Ohio area, customers are highly satisfied with ARTIMIS information accuracy and ease of use (Clemons et al, 1999). More than 99% of those surveyed reported they benefited from: avoiding traffic problems, saving time, reducing frustration, and arriving at destinations on time (Clemons et al, 1999). In addition, 65% of users reported they would be willing to pay for the service (Clemons et al, 1999). Battelle et al (2000) reported that for Arizona Interstate traveler and Tourist Information System, 78% of travelers on I-40 were aware of at least one deployed ATIS component. The report also found that over 50% of travelers interviewed agreed or strongly agreed that the traveler information they received made their travel more efficient, and over 70% of those who received information over the Internet thought the information beneficial. Toppen et al (2002) concluded in a report that ATIS users who are unfamiliar with the routes arrived at their destination punctually 79% of the time; while without ATIS, those drivers arrived punctually 42% of the time.

9.1.3. Aging population and limitation of the existing literature

Most literature discusses the rising popularity and advantages of ATIS from surveys throughout the country; however, little is mentioned about how ATIS could serve seniors. While there is literature that examines the aging of the population, only limited literature discusses the aging population in regard to traveler information systems.

Skinner and Stearns (1999) indicate that, due to the decrease of morbidity rate and the maturing of the baby boomers (those who were born between 1946 and 1964), the U.S. is experiencing population aging. Skinner and Stearns (1999) define aging in terms of demographics as an increase in the mean age of the entire population, or an increase in the relative proportion of older persons. Since 1900, the number of older adults in the population has increased eleven times, compared to only a three-time increase for those under age 65. According to the U.S. Census data, older adults numbered 33.5 million, or 12.8% of the population in 1995; by the year 2020, this age group is estimated to total 53.2 million, or 16.5 percent of the population; by 2030, 1 in 5 Americans will be older than 65 (Department of Transportation, 1997). Figure 9.1 shows the actual and projected growth of the U.S. population by age categories, according to Skinner and Stearns (1999). This figure suggests that there will

147

be over 20 million people aged 65 to 69 by the year 2030 and around 18 million people aged 70 to 74 by that year. The people at the age of 65 to 74 are still an important part of the driving population (Henk and Kuhn, 2000). As a result of this population aging, the regular shape of the age pyramid shifts to more of a balloon shape, with a much bigger top than the regular pyramid top. The average age of the population as well as the average driving age becomes older and moves upward in the age pyramid, as compared to the regular more pyramidal shape.

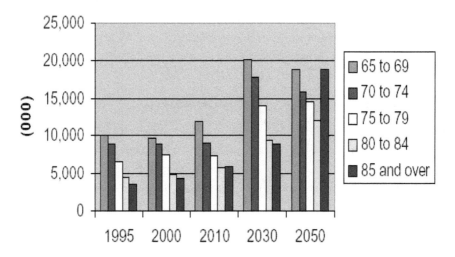

Figure 9.1 Actual and Projected Growth of the U.S. Population by Age Categories.
Source: Skinner and Stearns, 1999.

The aging of the population means that there will be more senior travelers and there will be an increase in the number and percentage of older drivers among the entire population. When considering the aging population in the field of transportation, scholars have explored the continuing need for seniors to travel and characteristics of their travel behavior. Skinner and Stearns (1999) point out that older persons still need mobility, not just for essential needs like

148

shopping, but also for social interactions, such as maintaining friendship. "Mobility" is used, in this context, to include trip making (Skinner and Stearns, 1999). As for senior people's travel behavior, Skinner and Stearns (1999) indicate that older people usually travel in the afternoon. Data offered by the Federal Highway Administration's (FHWA) <u>Older Driver Highway Design Handbook</u> show a higher risk of accidents involving older travelers.

9.2. Research Hypotheses

The ATIS seems to be an effective traveler information system for citizen's mobility. In the meantime, the population in this country is experiencing a demographic shift, and the aging of the population makes the travel safety of the elderly more and more crucial. Therefore, it is meaningful to explore whether retired seniors have unique travel behavior which can be served by ATIS.

Although research has investigated ATIS and the aging population separately, little addresses ATIS in regard to the aging population. This paper is designed to bridge the gap and test the following hypotheses:

- Seniors have unique travel behavior and this unique behavior requires ATIS.

- Compared with other current traveler information systems -- radio and TV traffic reports and in-vehicle automated navigation systems -- ATIS more effectively accommodates seniors' travel needs, which means that ATIS offer the information older travelers need, in a way that is easy for the elderly to access, and that they are well aware of and accept ATIS.

9.3 Methodology

This section introduces the methodology, data, and defines some key terms. It is worth noting again the complication of definitions of seniors . In most literature is 65 and above. However, some literature defined older ages in a different way. In this book, seniors and older people are defined as those who aged 62 and above particularly in the case of discussing retirees and using Public Use Micro Sample data for empirical analyses. When using the methodology as interpretative studies, this book would have to use the common definitions used in previous literature.

9.3.1 Methodology and Data

To analyze the above research questions, the methodology this paper uses includes data interpretation, descriptive statistics, and GIS mapping. It first examines seniors' driving safety by interpreting statistics of driving capability found by the U.S. FHWA (1998) and interpreting data of fatality rate provided by the U.S. Department of Transportation (1997). After interpreting data from Skinner and Stearns (1999) for elders' travel schedule, it further explores older people's travel mode choice by using data from National Household Travel Survey (NHTS) post-9/11 data.

As the integration of two national travel surveys: the Federal Highway Administration-sponsored Nationwide Personal Transportation Survey (NPTS) and the Bureau of Transportation Statistics-sponsored American Travel Survey, the NPTS is a national survey collecting data from a nationally representative sample of approximately a total of 66,000 households from April 2001 through May 2002, using Computer-Assisted Telephone Interviewing technology. The sample is composed of the civilian, non-institutionalized population of the United States and the NPTS survey data is expanded to provide national estimates of daily and long-distance trips. Demographic data as well as travel modes and behavior data are included.

After sorting data by age (older aged is defined as 65 or above), this study tabulated the daily trips elders versus younger travelers travel by owned vehicle and by taking public transit system in the metropolitan statistic areas (MSA). The reason metropolitan areas are used is that there is a higher density of residents, including elders, and there are more travel mode alternatives other than driving personal vehicles in metropolitan areas. After adjusting the sample data with personal-level weights, this paper mapped elders' and younger people's daily trip data by either using private owned vehicle or taking public transportation at the MSA level to visualize and compare the regional variations of the travel mode choice among elders versus younger travelers.

In order to analyze the characteristics of ATIS information, this paper compares and contrasts ATIS with other traveler information systems. Based on seniors' travel behavior, this

150

comparison and contrast is made through the following aspects of information offered by ATIS and broadcasting traveler information systems: availability, details, specificity, extensiveness, and customization. Between ATIS and the new automated in-vehicle navigation systems, this paper compares the difference of cost and the system accessibility to seniors.

The Discussion part of the paper calculated a simple correlation between age and the Internet access using NPTS data. Data offered by Henk and Kuhn (2000) about technology familiarity and usage is also cited to further support my analysis. All the data discusses a possible limitation ATIS has for senior users.

9.3.2 Definitions

In this chapter, the terms *older, senior,* and *elderly,* are defined chronologically and apply to people aged 65 or over, which is consistent with the definition by the U.S. Census (Department of Transportation, 1997). Most studies, including those cited in this paper, also use this definition. Accordingly, the term *younger* applies to people aged up to 65. Although Henk and Kuhn (2000) define "older" as age 55 or over, their younger drivers, represented as USAA responders, also include people between age 55 and 64.

The term *travel* generally refers to driving personal vehicles. Traveling by air, ship, or foot is not addressed. Since public transportation is not always available and since driving requires more attention, this paper addresses *travel* as driving in most contexts.

The term *ATIS* refers to the traveler information accessed via the Internet or telephone. The information ATIS offers generally refers to the *pre-route* traveler information, considering older travelers' reduced driving capability. In this context, in-vehicle automated navigation systems are not included in the category of ATIS because they basically offer *en-route* information.

9.4 Seniors' Unique Travel Behavior

An aging travel population means that the current traveler information systems need to give more of their service focus to senior travelers. Thus, it is necessary to investigate whether

ATIS meets senior travelers' needs. Consequently, it is necessary to first explore the travel behavior of seniors in terms of whether their traveling capability is similar to younger travelers, whether they travel as safely as younger travelers, whether they still need to drive after retirement, and whether they travel with similar schedules and purposes as younger travelers.

Travel behavior includes traveling capacity, need for travel, width of travel choices, travel purposes, and travel schedules. This part addresses seniors' travel behavior in terms of the above aspects.

9.4.1 Reduced Traveling Capability

Seniors have reduced driving capability. With increasing age, seniors experience decreased vision and hearing and slower mental response and decision-making (shown in Appendix 9.2). These reduced driving capabilities result in more accidents and higher crash rates, compared to younger drivers. Further, crash rates of older drivers are not evenly distributed across the various types of crashes. The sharpest increases of driving crash rates with age occur at intersections and crossing-path situations (Department of Transportation, 1997). Right- and left-turn and lane changes, particularly in urban areas, require complex maneuvers to avoid opposing traffic, which is difficult for senior drivers with reduced driving capability. Table 9.1 presents data on older drivers' decreased vision, slower response, and a higher risk of driving across intersections. Table 9.2 lists dangerous situations at intersections, such as identifying lighting, pavement markings, number of left-turn lanes, width of lanes, and other signs and signals. Senior drivers are also over-involved in accidents at stop signs (Department of Transportation, 1997, p29). Seniors' reduced driving capability results in difficulty in perceiving and judging the dynamics of traffic movement and performing cognitive tasks with time constraints. Consequently, more accidents occur at stop signs.

Table 9.1 Driver Activities Becoming More Difficult with Age

* Reading street signs in town--7%

* Driving across an intersection------------------------------------ 21%

* Finding the beginning of a left-turn lane at an intersection------------ 20%

* Making a left turn at an intersection------------------------------19%

* Following pavement markings------------------------------------17%

* Responding to traffic signals------------------------------------12%

Source: Federal Highway Administration, 1998.

Table 9.2 Highway Features Becoming More Difficult for Drivers with Age

* Lighting at intersections--62%

* Pavement marking at intersections---------------------------------- 57%

* Number of left-turn lanes at an intersection------------------------ 55%

* Width of travel lanes--51%

* Concrete lane guides (raised channelization) for turns at intersections--47%

* Size of traffic signals--42%

Source: Federal Highway Administration, 1998.

Senior travelers' reduced vision and hearing result in a delayed response times for reacting to traffic in traffic flow where all the drivers are required to drive at a similar speed. Moreover, senior travelers need longer time to make decisions. If senior travelers are familiar with road information, such as street signs, number of left-turn lanes, pavement markings, width of lanes, they can better prepare for reaction to changes in traffic flow. Consequently, equipping senior travelers with accurate traveler information before they travel can ensure them enough time to react to traffic and thus mitigate the driving risk caused by reduced driving capability. Therefore, developing traveler information systems is beneficial.

By driving less, slower, and more carefully, senior drivers can also mitigate the risk of accidents caused by their decreased sensory-motor skills that are primary for motor vehicle operation. Cerreli (1998) indicates that on a per-licensed driver basis, older drivers have fewer absolute numbers of crashes and have a low crash rate, compared to other age groups. However, on a per-mile driven basis, older drivers have relatively higher rates of crash involvement. Moreover, fatal crashes increase steadily after the age of 65 (as shown in Figure 9.2). The U-shape fatality rate starts turning up around age 60 and appears almost vertical by age 80.

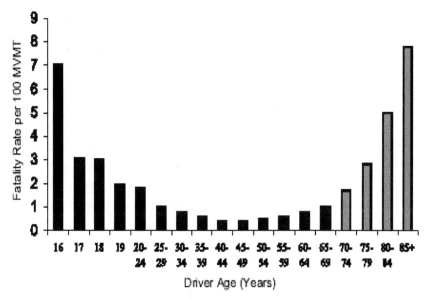

Figure 9.2 National Driver Fatality Rates by Age.
Based on 1996 National Highway Traffic Safety Administration
NHTSA) data; MVMT = million vehicle miles traveled.

Source: Department of Transportation, 1997.

9.4.2 More Flexible Travel Schedules for Seniors

Seniors have a similar need to travel as younger people, but their travel behavior is different. Because of retirement or reduced need to commute to work, older travelers tend to have more flexible travel schedules and more free time. Without the need to commute to work, senior travelers usually choose to travel during non-commuting hours to avoid heavy traffic. Skinner and Stearns (1999) document that travel for this group is mainly concentrated in the afternoon. Also, due to reduced driving capability, older operators do not drive proportionately as much at night (p11).

In general, seniors have more freedom to choose their travel schedules. However, seniors' travel schedules cannot be completely flexible in trip timing. Some travel demand occurs at specific times to manage scheduled events, such as doctor visits and concerts (Skinner and Stearns, 1999).

9.4.3 Seniors' Continued Need for Driving & Their Unique Travel Purposes

Seniors' more flexible travel schedules do not necessarily mean they travel less. It is interesting to examine seniors' travel mode. Similar to younger people, seniors still need to travel due to their demand for goods, services, social interactions, and perhaps work. Since land use in the U.S. is dispersed and activity centers are not collocated, most people remain in their original communities after retirement (Treas, 1995). As a result, the older cohort may increasingly find themselves living in areas where shopping, entertainment, and socializing may be linked only by roads and may often lack public transportation (Skinner & Stearns, 1999). In addition, for some senior people, even though public transportation is available to them, they still choose to drive because they have been accustomed to driving for a long time and they prefer driving.

Calculating and mapping MSA data from NHTS post-9/11 data, Figures 10.3 through 10.6 contrast the daily trips made by private owned vehicles and by public transit between younger and older travelers. Comparing Figure 9.3 to Figurer 10.4, older travelers (shown as blue pies in Figure 9.3) tend to travel by owned vehicle less than the younger ones (shown as red pies in Figure 9.4): a bigger proportion of elders never use private owned vehicle as a daily travel mode and generally a higher proportion of younger travelers than older ones travel by owned vehicle more than 6 times a day. This may relate to the fact that elders have less need of commuting to work. On the other hand, since elders still have various travel needs, their reduced driving capacity may make some of them switch to alternative travel modes like the public transportation system in metropolitan areas. Comparing Figure 5 to 6, older travelers, however, also tend to use public transit less than the younger ones—there tend to be a smaller proportion of elders (shown as blue pies in Figure 9.5) who never use public transit than the proportion of the younger ones (shown as red pies in Figure 9.6); fewer elders take public transit once or more than once as daily trips. Appendix 9.3 also shows that 98.44% of older travelers never use public

156

transit as a daily travel mode, while only 97.57% of younger travelers never use transit as a daily travel mode. Please note that the data collected and mapped here is at the MSA level, which means people in the survey are basically accessible to public transit due to living in the metropolitan areas. Although elders tend to have more difficulty in driving due to reduced driving capacity and even they have such alternative travel mode as public transportation system as options, public transit does not show higher popularity among elders than among the younger ones.

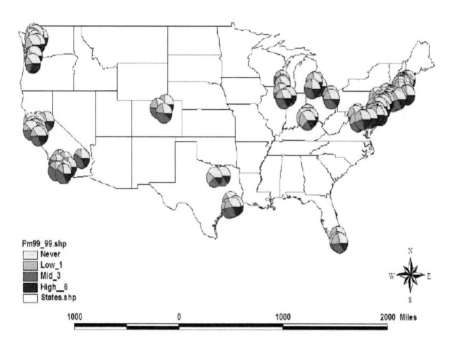

Figure 9.3 Elders' Daily Travel by Owned Vehicles, MSA, 2002
Data source: National Household Travel Survey post-9/11 data.

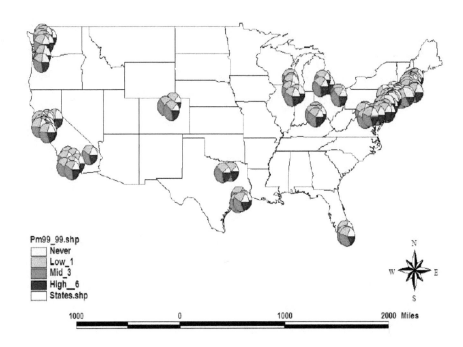

Figure 9.4 Younger Travelers' Daily Travel by Owned Vehicles, MSA, 2002

Data source: National Household Travel Survey post-9/11 data.

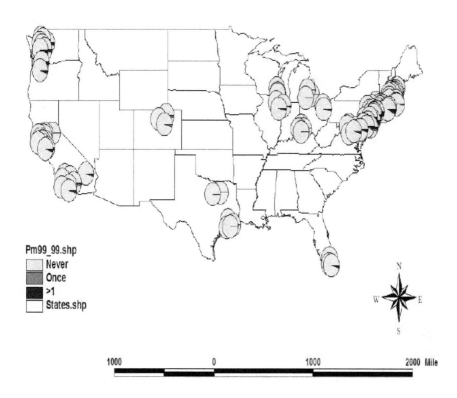

Figure 9.5 Elders' Daily Travel by Public Transit, MSA, 2002

Data source: National Household Travel Survey post-9/11 data.

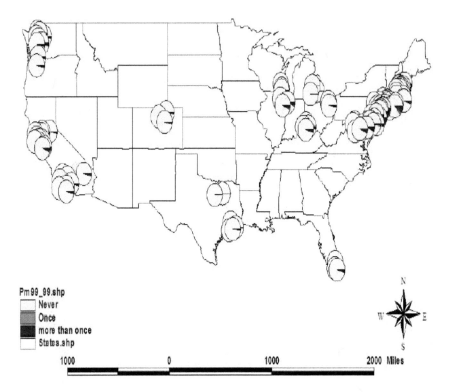

Figure 9.6 Younger Travelers' Daily Travel by Public Transit, MSA, 2002

Data source: National Household Travel Survey post-9/11 data.

In addition, some seniors travel for a long distance more frequently than younger people. There is a highly selective interstate migration of elderly people. The elderly who migrate tend to be the younger elderly and have relatively higher incomes (Litwak and Longino, n.d.). Those younger elderly who also have higher incomes choose leisure travel more frequently because they have more free time than when they were young and working.

9.5 Solutions for Seniors' Travel Behavior

Seniors' unique travel behavior requires unique approaches to accommodate their travel. As the NHTS data presented earlier already shows, public transit lacks popularity among elders in metropolitan areas; for non-urban areas, public transportation is not available everywhere. Thus, just developing public transportation is not enough to meet older travelers' needs.

Developing traveler information systems is another way to meet seniors' travel needs. Traveler information prepares travelers with more road-related information, reduces the response time to recognize and react to unfamiliar traffic information, and thus improves travel safety, which is particularly beneficial to senior travelers. Traveler information can also help travelers choose a safer travel environment or route before traveling.

Traditional traveler information systems, i.e. radio and TV broadcasts, only offer brief traffic reports concentrating on basic road conditions of major routes during rush hour (Oski, n.d.), instead of extensive route-specific traveler information available at all times, which the aging population really needs. ATIS can make up for the shortcoming of the broadcast traveler information systems and thus, meet senior travelers' unique needs. Moreover, ATIS do not only improve driving safety, but also increase the efficiency of taking public transportation.

In general, although none of the traveler information systems are designed to especially serve senior travelers, ATIS has a better and larger capacity to meet senior travelers needs, compared to other traveler information systems.

9.6 ATIS and Senior Travelers

This section analyzes the relationship and interaction between ATIS and senior travelers through comparing ATIS to other traveler information systems. The advantage of ATIS is evident due to the flexibility information technology offers in the "Knowledge Economy". This flexibility is particularly helpful to senior travelers.

9.6.1 ATIS vs. Radio and TV Traffic Reports

Compared with broadcasting traveler information systems, ATIS has the following distinct advantages to serve seniors' unique travel behavior: ATIS information is available at any time; offers more detailed information; customizes information through interaction with users.

The level of availability

ATIS offers information at all times, which meets seniors' travel schedules. As mentioned above, without the need to commute to work, seniors have more flexible schedules which tend to focus on non-commuting hours and thus for a safer travel environment. However, as Orski mentioned, radio and TV traffic programs report traffic information frequently during commuting hours. *Commuting hours* are normally defined as 6:00 a.m. to 9:00 a.m. and 4:00 p.m. to 6:30 p.m.. During non-commuting hours, radio and TV traveler information systems report much less. In terms of the information availability, broadcasting traveler information systems aim to serve younger citizens. Since ATIS traffic information is available at all times and is updated frequently, travelers can obtain route-specific information at anytime, as long as they have a phone or Internet access. This level of availability of ATIS information better meets senior travelers' needs. Consequently, older travelers can find traffic information during non-commuting travel hours as well as during high-density commuting periods, and they need not wait for radio or TV reports.

Quality of content

Seniors' travel purposes are diverse, which requires extensive, detailed and specific traveler information. This requirement cannot be achieved by traditional broadcast based traveler information systems, but it can be fulfilled by ATIS. As addressed earlier, with strong technological and institutional support, ATIS offer real time information which is route-specific and extensive, while radio and TV only offer brief and simple traffic reports. In order for the broadcasting industry to operate well, radio and TV have to "bundle" the brief traveler information with newscasts, talk shows, music and other programs (Orski, n.d.). This situation nuances that it is not possible for radio and TV traffic reports to be very specific. Commuters' travel purposes are relatively focused on a simple work or home bound trip, while seniors travel for doctor's appointment, visiting friends and relatives, shopping, and leisure. With such varied

162

travel purposes, the brief radio and TV traffic reports, mostly focused on limited major routes during rush hour, cannot meet seniors' travel needs.

The much more extensive information ATIS offers can be tailored toward older travelers' diverse needs. For example, since senior travelers tend to have more difficulty at intersection or merging, if more information about road conditions can be given at intersection and lane merging areas, it would help senior travelers reduce traffic risks.

Interaction & customization of information

ATIS uses the phones or the Internet to transmit information. This fact creates the possibility of interactive communication between the services and customers, which would be extremely beneficial for older travelers. Considering their diverse travel purposes, flexible travel schedules, and reduced travel capability, customized information will help senior travelers obtain more personalized information for their travel and achieve safer travel. Different from traditional radio and TV information delivery, which is one-directional and customers cannot inquire in detail or give feedback, ATIS' interactive approaches for information have the capacity to receive customers' immediate feedback and to offer customized information. The type of interactive information includes weather, time, route choices, construction, new signs and markings, and necessary precautions that should be taken. Currently, most ATIS products provide email or telephone numbers for customer services, which can at least provide customers' feedback and improve ATIS services to better meet customers' needs.

Table 9.3 briefly concludes the above comparison between the traveler information offered by radio and TV traffic reports and by ATIS, considering seniors' needs. The first column lists the characteristics of traveler information. The second and third columns compare the radio and TV traveler information with ATIS information, in terms of the level of availability, quality of content, transmitting devices, and interaction and customization. The last column lists the characteristics of traveler information senior travelers require. The table shows that the contents in the third and the last column are very similar. Thus, Table 9.3 suggests that ATIS information serves senior travelers' needs quite well.

Table 9.3 Traveler Information System Comparison – Radio & TV vs. ATIS

Characteristics of Traveler Information	Radio & TV Traveler Information	ATIS Information	Senior Travelers' Needs for Traveler information
Amount of Availability	Commuting hours Bundled with other programs	At all times	At all times Especially in the afternoon
Quality of Content	Brief Simple	Route-specific Up-to-minute Extensive Detailed	Specific Detailed Extensive Customized
Transmitting Devices	Radio TV	Telephones The Internet	Telephones Radio TV The Internet
Interaction & Customization	Information reception No interaction No information customization	Two-directional interaction Customization of information	Interactive communication Customization of information

9.6.2 ATIS vs. In-Vehicle Automated Navigation Systems

Considering seniors' reduced driving capability, ATIS pre-route information available via telephone or the Internet is superior to the new advanced en-route information provided by in-vehicle automated navigation systems. For seniors, due to decreased vision, hearing, and attention to driving, it is distractive and thus, extremely dangerous, to check the in-vehicle navigation display while driving. In addition, due to their reduced memory functions and slower learning processes (Pawlovich, 2002), it would be difficult for them to master the new technology. Contrarily, ATIS pre-route information can familiarize senior drivers with the necessary road-related information before driving and thus, improve en-route safety.

Also, the new navigation systems are designed for drivers, whereas some older travelers take public transportation. ATIS information serves both drivers and those who use public transportation. In addition, these new systems will need several years of evolution for the cost to lower and to become more technically mature (Booz Allen and Hamilton, 1994), whereas ATIS information is basically free to users.

ATIS shows its superiority to serve senior travelers in comparison to not only the traditional broadcasting traveler information systems, but also the new in-vehicle automated navigation systems. This superiority determines the significance of ATIS for the travel safety of the aging population.

9.7 Stronger Acceptance of ATIS from Older Drivers

As interpreted above, ATIS can meet older travelers' needs effectively because of the more extensive, customized, and continuously available ATIS information. Therefore, ATIS are more readily accepted by older than by younger drivers, as supported by data presented in the following tables from Henk and Kuhn (2000). Based on surveys distributed among five winter residential communities and among employees of a local large employer in McAllen, Pharr and San Benito, Texas, Henk and Kuhn (2000) get the results in following tables. Table 9.4 and 5 indicate that ATIS information has a stronger effect on older drivers than younger ones (represented as USAA responders in Table 9.4 and 5). Table 9.4 shows that, in response to ATIS information, a much higher percentage of older than younger drivers are willing to change their travel behavior. These changes of travel behavior include changing travel mode, changing departure time, and trip cancellation. For example, after obtaining ATIS information, 11% of younger drivers (USAA responders) were willing to change departure time, whereas 48 % of the older drivers would change departure time; 2% of younger drivers would change travel mode, whereas 8% of the older drivers would do so; 1% of younger drivers would cancel trip, whereas 7% of older drivers would cancel a trip. Although Table 9.4 also shows that a slightly smaller percentage of older drivers than younger drivers would change routes and a higher percentage of older than younger drivers would make no change, these percentage differences are much smaller, as compared to other percentage differences shown in the same table.

165

Table 9.4 Response to ATIS Information

If you had access to accurate travel information, what would be your typical response upon hearing of a major delay on your planned route?	
Younger Drivers (USAA)-- Responses (Percentage, %)	
Change travel mode	2 (2%)
Change departure time	15 (11%)
Change route	116 (86%)
Cancel trip	1 (1%)
Make no changes	1 (1%)
Older Drivers-- Responses (Percentage, %)	
Change travel mode	42 (8%)
Change departure time	237 (48%)
Change route	362 (73%)
Cancel trip	34 (7%)
Make no changes	19 (4%)

Source: Henk and Kuhn, 2000.

Table 9.5 shows the result from participants' rating of ATIS. A smaller percentage of older drivers than USAA responders, or younger drivers, express their strong disagreement on the benefit of ATIS. A higher percentage of older drivers than USAA responders strongly agree that ATIS decreases stress and helps them to know what to expect for the road condition and that ATIS allows them to adjust their schedules.

Table 9.5 Benefits of ATIS

	Strongly disagree	Agree	Strongly agree
Young Drivers (USAA)-- Reponses (Percentage, %)			
Decreases stress I know what to expect	11 (8%)	62 (45%)	64 (47%)
Allows me to adjust my schedule	12 (9%)	61 (45%)	62 (46%)
Saves time because I can alter my route	4 (3%)	41 (31%)	89 (66%)
Older Drivers-- Reponses (Percentage, %)			
Decreases stress I know what to expect	13 (3%)	166 (44%)	203 (53%)
Allows me to adjust my schedule	15 (4%)	139 (35%)	245 (61%)
Saves time because I can alter my route	8 (3%)	126 (42%)	164 (55%)

Source: Henk and Kuhn, 2000.

10.8 Limitations of this Study

Limitations of this study has two sources. On e is from the limitations of data and the other is due to the limitation of current ATIS technology.

9.8.1 Limitations of Data

The NHTS data used in this study is still a sample data. Although personal-level weights are considered in the tabulation and calculation for the estimation at the national level, sample estimation cannot fully predict the population and certain inaccuracies is possible. In addition, this study also cited data from several other sources. A certain data may be applicable for its original study, but the calibrations of different data sources may be inconsistent. For example, the age definition of the Herk and Kuhn (2000) survey for elders is defined as 55 and above. However, due to the limitation of the data availability, this data is the closest evidence for elders' strong awareness and acceptance of ATIS.

9.8.2 Limitations of ATIS

Along with ATIS' superiority to other traveler information systems in serving an aging population, it also has source limitation. ATIS uses phones or the Internet to deliver traveler information. Phone access is generally not a problem in this society, but Internet access is still not so common among senior travelers. Henk and Kuhn (2000) noted that seniors' had limited familiarity and use of technology. As mentioned by the Department of Transportation (1997), technological complexity confuses or burdens many elderly operators. Using NHTS data, a negative correlation (-0.3958) is shown between web access and being aged 65 or over (Table 9.6), which indicates that the elderly tend to have less Internet access.

Table 9.6 Correlation between Being An Elderly and the Internet Access

	Internet Access	Aged 65 or over
Internet Access	1.0000	
Aged 65 or over	-0.3958	1.0000
Observation= 29736.		

Data source: National Household Travel Survey post-9/11 data.

A survey research by Henk and Kuhn (2000) also evidenced the limited Internet access among the elderly. As shown in Appendix 9.4, for the familiarity with technology, 100% of younger drivers respond as being familiar with the Internet or World Wide Web, while only 23% of older drivers state that they are familiar; 97 % of younger responders claim access to the Internet, while only 18 % of older drivers have access to the Internet; 32% of younger drivers use the Internet, while only 7% of older drivers mention use of the Internet. In addition, Appendix 9.4 indicates that a smaller percentage of older drivers use radios and a higher percentage of senior drivers use televisions for traveler information.

Since access to the Internet is much more deficient for older drivers, their usage of ATIS will be more heavily restricted to phones. Thus, it is necessary to make Internet access to ATIS information more elderly friendly. However, as the population ages, more and more people in the category of younger drivers at present will join the older drivers and the percentage of the Internet usage among older drivers will correspondingly increase. In the meantime, some older drivers might also learn how to use the Internet. Then, there is possibility that Internet usage will not be a severe constraint for ATIS information access in the following years.

9.8.3 Other Source of Intelligent Transportation Systems

This study does not address the role of other sources of intelligent transportation systems to improve elders' travel safety. Although other intelligent transportation systems, such as assistive technologies and universal design, do not necessarily belong to my definition of ATIS that emphasizing the pre-route information transmitted by the Internet and telephone systems, it is worthy mentioning that they are also critical to improve elders mobility. For example, using bigger fonts and more eye-catching colors for road signs and adding voice recognition system to the in-vehicle automated information system could effectively help seniors timely recognize road designs and improve travel safety. All these efforts, as well as catering ATIS for seniors' travel needs would be an increasingly important issue for an aging population.

9.9 Conclusion

The aging of the U.S. population results in proportionally more senior travelers. Seniors still have the need to travel and their travel behavior is unique. First, they experience reduced driving capability, which result in higher crash rates than younger drivers on a per-mile driven basis. Moreover, their travel schedules and purposes are more diverse. Although older travelers tend to use private owned vehicles less than the younger ones due to reduced need to commute to work, public transportation has not shown popularity among the elderly. This situation requires an effective traveler information system to offer more detailed and customized information catering to seniors' travel needs because effective traveler information can mitigate the higher risks of accidents resulting from seniors' reduced driving capability. ATIS has the capability to satisfy this requirement.

With strong technological and institutional support for the quality of information, ATIS is superior to conventional radio and TV traffic reports for meeting older travelers' needs. The information it offers is route-specific, detailed and available at all times over telephones or the Internet, while radio and TV traffic reports are generally brief and concentrated to commuting hours. The capability of ATIS information caters to seniors' more diverse travel purposes and schedules, as compared to younger travelers. In addition, the information that ATIS offers can also be customized to the various needs of older travelers by possible interaction between its services and customers, which is more difficult for radio and TV traffic reports to achieve.

ATIS pre-route information is also superior to the en-route travel information offered by new automated in-vehicle navigation systems, considering senior travelers. As the age of travelers increases, there is a decline in vision, hearing, and attention. So, using an in-vehicle navigation system increases distractions and will make driving more dangerous. Also, these new navigation systems are more costly.

A survey data shows that ATIS receives a strong acceptance from older drivers than younger ones. This fact provides support for the statement that ATIS has advantages in serving senior travelers.

In addition to data limitations, ATIS also has disadvantages for older drivers, such as senior travelers' limited Internet access to its information. This disadvantage is declining because more and more seniors are using the Internet. Additionally, the telephone is another way to access ATIS, which more fully guarantees older travelers' accessibility to its information.

With the aging of the population, designing a traveler information system to cater to the needs of older travelers will not only help create a better travel environment for the older population, but also society as a whole. However, since there is little literature addressing ATIS in regard to senior travelers, more research exploring this issue should be undertaken.

In addition, ATIS should further develop its services to meet older travelers' needs, particularly for the interaction with users. Currently, ATIS offers telephone numbers and email addresses for customer services. However, telephone hotlines may be busy and email messages may not be responded to immediately. Since ATIS has the technological and institutional capacity to achieve interaction with customers, more possible interaction should be fulfilled. For

170

instance, using Internet Forum and Instant Message to realize dialogues with customers at anytime would offer immediate customized information to senior travelers, which would be extremely beneficial to those who are seeking immediate help.

Part VI Conclusion

Aging has been an unpleasant word implying a slowing down mechanism, weakening functions, and ailing image. In the aging society, the anti-aging concept, products and services are gaining enormous popularity. Additionally, elderly care and so called "adult daycare" and long term care become emerging business opportunities. The underlying assumption of all the above associations with aging is that seniors are the burden of the society and they compose a source of crises.

The aging society, even like the one that the United States has, has been predicted to result in potential labor and fiscal crises. An increasingly large seniors' population brings about concerns and worries on whether the aging society will constrain economic growth due to the increasingly large consumer population of seniors and the relatively shrinking producer population of younger people.

It is true that biological aging process is simultaneously a waning process of human body system. To this extent, aging is not a pleasant situation. However, the current aging society is experiencing the "Knowledge Economy" in which experience, skills, knowledge, and social ties have dominant powers for economic growth. In this information technology based "Knowledge Economy", numerous new technology products and services could assist seniors to achieve an extended life experience. The rising importance of knowledge and social capitals and the emerging assisted technology are both reducing seniors' physical constraints to be further involved in socioeconomic activities. Also, with better medical and health conditions, seniors are living longer. With the average retirement age at 62 in the United States, most seniors are facing a long retirement period. Yet, there is still so much for seniors to enjoy, not just a retirement life that totally detaches them from their beloved career or other social goals.

More importantly, the knowledge and social capital driven "Knowledge Economy" grants seniors more power and opportunities to express their ambition. Seniors' cumulative skills, experience, social ties, and mentoring capability become vital factors that drive economic growth. Seniors, therefore, can continue playing powerful roles in various socioeconomic activities. Compared to the younger cohorts, seniors even have unique competitive advantages— their experience, skills, social ties, and patience generally excel those who are younger. In this case, instead of standing aside taking the purely social-wealth consumers' role, seniors can be

173

dynamic players of the aging but knowledge driven economy. In some circumstances, such as specific economic sectors and occupations, seniors can even be a more vigorous power pushing and leading the economy to grow.

It is in the "Knowledge Economy" that aging does not just mean crises, but also opportunities. Aging does not simply mean slowdown of economic growth, instead, if gasping the opportunities, an aging society could be powerful economy with unprecedented growth momentum. This book therefore explored the dynamics between the aging society and the "Knowledge Economy" and attempted to identify the opportunities this aging society could bring.

Summary of Findings

This book started with introducing and interpreting what the "Knowledge Economy" is. To describe the "Knowledge Economy", Chapter 1 explained the economic shift from the previous "Fordist Economy" to the "Knowledge Economy" through interpreting economic growth theories and indicated the new factors to growth are knowledge, innovation, and human capital.

To delineate the possible opportunities the "Knowledge Economy" could bring, Chapter 2 introduced a new regional economic growth framework that fundamentally differs from the previous one. With the information technology as the base of the "Knowledge Economy", distance decay factor is not as dominant as before. Spatial diffusion promoted by the diffusing information technology becomes more possible. As a result, the traditional core-periphery regional economic growth model is shifting to a polycentric regional economic structure. The advantage of the new polycentric regional development structure can not only give the peripheral areas more opportunities to growth, but also ease the core city center's diseconomies of scale. Integratively, this polycentric model can spur a more balanced development of a region and can more possibly fulfill a region's potential from every corner. This polycentric regional development model not only expands knowledge spillovers and fosters more entrepreneurship and opportunities, but also requires entrepreneurial initiatives to achieve its prosperity.

Eventually, in the "Knowledge Economy", the polycentric regional development model is not only a network with economic hubs, but also a network of entrepreneurship hubs. This network has the potential to efficiently spread knowledge and fertilize opportunities.

After describing and analyzing trends in the "Knowledge Economy" in Part II, Part III focused on describing the demographic trend of aging and analyzing the implications of aging. Chapter 3 used Thompson's demographic transition model to describe the long-run demographic trends in the United States. Aging in the United States, like in many other countries, is related to baby boomers, but the baby boomer generation is not the only or not even a major source of population aging in the United States, based on data from the U.S. Census historical population estimates and future population forecasts. Instead, aging is concluded in this chapter as a long-term trend that was not originated from the baby boomers and will not disappear with baby boomers' exit, unless major changes sourced from exogenous factors occur.

Chapter 4 first interpreted the implications of aging, i.e., the labor and fiscal crises aging could result in. Then, this chapter discussed several possible policy options to mitigate the aging related crises and eventually focused on seniors' labor force participation as a viable solution. This chapter further explained the disincentives and incentives for seniors to be involved in the labor force. The disincentives include the early retirement policies, individuals' unique situations and family needs, sufficient income and wealth for retirement, structural disincentives, and social stereotypes against seniors. The incentives for seniors to participate in the labor force include seniors' improved health conditions, needs for self-actualization, seniors' rich knowledge and social capital, and new innovative arrangement that allows for flexible work schedules.

Following the detailed discussions and interpretations on the "Knowledge Economy" and aging respectively in Parts II and III, Part IV further investigated seniors' employability and thus pondered the relationship between old age and occupation choice. Chapter 5 sought for theoretical answers to seniors' employability from the social gerontology theories. However, no clear clue was identified.

Chapter 6 preliminarily explored the industry mix of seniors' employment to investigate what sectors seniors tend to be concentrated in, once they are employed. This chapter found out that, based on the industry code used in the data of this chapter (*Profiles of Older Workers*), older workers tend to concentrated in the three "Knowledge Economy" related sectors—retail trade, financial insurance services and real estate, and services sectors, particularly for selective subsectors. However, this study can only be called preliminary and exploratory due to the limitations of the data. The sample size is small and the industry code used in this dataset differs from standard NAICS codes.

Chapter 7 therefore used a different dataset, a much more detailed and intensive dataset, Census PUMS, to directly investigate seniors' occupational choice and sectoral distribution. It found out that seniors are more likely to be self-employed, particularly in the knowledge-based sectors, and that elderly entrepreneurship is seniors' occupational choice. Seniors also have a lower wage-and-salary employment rates than the younger employed individuals. The binomial logit model estimation indicated that being of older age (62 and above) is associated with a higher propensity to entrepreneurship. Seniors can be entrepreneurs! The fact that seniors can achieve entrepreneurship, which is more demanding than average wage-and-salary jobs, and that older age is even associated with a higher propensity to entrepreneurship indicates that seniors can participate and be active players in the labor force.

After investigating the age myth, Part V examined the interactive relationship between the fundamental demographic shift and economic shift. i.e., aging and the "Knowledge Economy" respectively. Chapter 8 extended the entrepreneurship growth model that was used in the previous literature and developed a path analysis model to test elderly entrepreneurship's economic, labor, and fiscal roles. The empirical tests relied on data from the Census PUMS, Bureau of Labor Statistics, American Community Survey, and Social Security Administration and found out that elderly entrepreneurship has a strong association with metropolitan economic growth, state labor force size increase, and Social Security fund contribution. Interestingly, the impact of seniors' entrepreneurship on metropolitan economic growth is actually stronger than entrepreneurship from younger working-age people. It is worth noting that the empirical tests have certain limitations. The methodological and theoretical details were delineated in Zhang (2008).

Chapter 9 addressed the elderly-friendly environment the "Knowledge Economy" brings about through a case study in the usage of Advanced Traveler Information Systems (ATIS). ATIS refers to information technology based real time traffic alert and travel design systems.

176

Compared to other traveler information systems, this case study first examined seniors' unique travel behavior and needs and further found out that ATIS has unique advantages to cater for seniors travel behavior and needs. The advantages derive from the flexibility, real time availability, information details, and customization potentials of ATIS that traditional traveler information systems, i.e. radio and TV traffic reports, are not able to achieve. It also compared ATIS to the current in-vehicle automated navigation systems and found that the in-vehicle systems could be distractive for seniors. ATIS's elderly friendly functions can be evidenced by the survey data that was cited in this chapter. The survey shows that ATIS has a strong acceptance from older drivers.

Concluding Remarks

Based on this above chapters, the "Knowledge Economy" can be elderly friendly and can bring in many opportunities. With the diffusive information technology and therefore diffusive knowledge flow and entrepreneurship flow, the regional economic development could develop into a polycentric structure. With reduced location and physical constraints and with the social necessities to mitigate the aging related crises and the need to continue fulfilling career ambitions after retirement age, seniors can be a dynamic and unique power in the "Knowledge Economy" with their own competitive advantages. Their competitive advantages are their cumulated experience, skills, social ties, and their patience, guidance, and other virtues. The data cited in this book show that seniors are playing an active role in the "Knowledge Economy" through their employment concentration in selective knowledge-based sectors and though their entrepreneurship. Seniors' entrepreneurship not only can large push metropolitan economic growth, effectively enlarge the labor force size, and increase the Social Security fund contribution, their entrepreneurship has even a stronger impact on economic growth than entrepreneurship from the young. In this case, bringing seniors in the labor force could reenergize the economy.

We are standing at an exciting historical intersection: fundamental demographic shift to aging and fundamental economic shift to the "Knowledge Economy". In the "Knowledge

Economy", economic growth does not have to be subject to diminishing returns to scale that is determined by the characteristics of physical capital and labor; instead, an unprecedented nondiminishing, and even increasing return to scale is showing up, according to the new growth theory. This nondiminishing return, or even the increasing return, originates from the properties of knowledge capital. Also in this "Knowledge Economy", even the traditionally well accepted core-periphery regional development structure can be shifted to a polycentric mode, how is it impossible for seniors to play a uniquely and unprecedentedly powerful role in the "Knowledge Economy"? In this widely diffusive economy that is not much constrained by location and physical conditions, seniors does not have to retire around the age 62; instead, they could be as active as the young, and even more dynamic than the young. If we believe aging results in labor shortage, brining in more seniors in the labor force would change the labor shortage crisis to an opportunity. If we believe aging results in fiscal crisis, with more seniors in the labor force to contribute their wisdom, we will have more social wealth to conquer the crises. Eventually, seniors in the labor force could not just mitigate the aging related crises; instead, the under-discovered power from seniors could largely increase social wealth and thus result in more opportunities. In this sense, aging not necessarily implies crises to the society; aging can means just the opposite and brings in incredible opportunities to spur our economy to prosper.

Policy Implications

To involve more seniors in the workforce, it would be necessary to motivate both employers and seniors. To attract employers' support, it would be necessary to educate employers about potential workforce shortages and older people's productivity through various public avenues. To update seniors' skills to accommodate them who have been detached from the job market for a long time to be more valuable workforce participants, trainings that cater to the job requirements are necessary. Retrainings for seniors to continue their original jobs may be more cost-efficient than training for the unfamiliar new jobs. For those seniors who do not have enough motivation to return to work, particularly those with high levels of job skills, ensuring a positive working environment to remind them of life satisfaction gained from working would be helpful.

An accommodating working environment is also important. This accommodating environment includes a comfortable business culture, high respect toward seniors, flexible working schedule catering for older people's needs, allowing for teleworking, financial incentives such as various insurances, etc.

Policy initiatives to enhance senior labor force participation could include offering tax credits to reward both employers and senior workers for later retirement, removing early retirement incentives, organizing various job skill trainings and job hunting trainings, reimbursing certain training costs for older people, funding researches in this topic, increasing accessibility to various services through universal design and assisted technology, and advertising successful experiences. Although these policy efforts may be costly for the limited government revenue, those cost will generate larger economic and social returns in the long run by enlarging the work force, eliminating age discrimination, and enhancing social equity. However, promoting later retirement does not mean forcing older people to continue working after current retirement age. Delaying legal retirement age, cutting Medicare benefit, and reducing promised Social Security benefits would put older people into the situation of being taken advantaged of and thus jeopardize government credibility. With limited public funds, it is necessary to target funds on needs and redistribute wealth through various innovative approaches.

Since entrepreneurship is seniors' occupational choice and elderly entrepreneurship can push economic growth, enlarge the labor force size, and increase Social Security Fund contribution, developing elderly entrepreneurship would be a necessary policy direction to transfer aging related crises to opportunities. The elderly should first be included as the new focus and priority for entrepreneurship initiatives.

Government's tax incentive could be preferred to elderly entrepreneurs to encourage entrepreneurs to retain in the labor force and to encourage other seniors to be involved in more entrepreneurial activities. Government agencies, such as U.S. Administration on Aging and Small Business Administration, could design some social programs that relieve seniors from various social barriers (such as social discrimination and difficult working environment) to become entrepreneurs so that entrepreneurs after retirement age are more likely to remain entrepreneurs and other seniors who are interested in being an entrepreneur could be more possible to jump in. Government agencies could also design low cost or even free entrepreneurship workshops and forum programs to the elderly. For those who are senior and skilled in entrepreneurship, the programs can set them as examples; for those who have ideas but do not have enough knowledge, skills, or access to starting a business, necessary trainings on writing business plans, learning financial management, familiarizing with business starting procedures, and referring to the correct network would be very helpful. Other public policy efforts could include mass media, enterprise incubating efforts, and research supports.

Underpowered groups, females and minority seniors (such as Blacks and Natives) deserve more attention in elderly entrepreneurship policies, since those groups are less likely to be entrepreneurs, according to Chapter 7. This situation is particularly critical for the elderly. Among the elderly population, female population takes a bigger proportion than males. One way to empower them is through organizing unions and connecting them to appropriate network. Policy programs that help them to identify and market their own uniqueness would be extremely enlightening. This effort could benefit both younger and elderly underrepresented entrepreneurial groups, i.e. female and minority entrepreneurs.

Based on this book, the "Knowledge Economy" not only provide a fostering environment for seniors to continue their economic activities and labor force participation, if they choose to, it also improves seniors' life quality through the information based "footloose" technology, not just for assisted technology, but even in traveler information systems. Seniors have also been found to be more concentrated in knowledge-based sectors. However, for many seniors, access to and familiarity with information based technology are still with certain level of difficulty, Therefore, customizing the current information technology to incorporate seniors' needs and thus to further fulfill seniors' potential contribution and ambition to the society would possibly transfer fundamentally the aging-related crises to opportunities with extra and skilled labor and brainpower. It is in this specific situation that aging does not necessarily bring only crises, aging could actually bring unprecedented opportunities!

Bibliography

AARP, n.d.. "Employment and Income Security in an Aging World: A U.S. Perspective." Retrieved from World Wide Web on August 28, 2005 at http://www.aarp.org/research/work/employment/a2003-02-11-russell.html.

Achenbaum, W. A., and V. C. Bengtson (1994). "Re-engaging the Disengagement Theory of Aging: Or the History and Assessment of Theory Development in Gerontology". *The Gerontologist*, 1994, 34, p. 756-763.

Acs, Z., Audretsch D. B. (1990) *Innovation and Small Firms*. MIT Press, Cambridge, MA

Acs, Z, Audretsch D, Braunerhjelm P, Carlsson B (2004) "The missing link: The knowledge filter entrepreneurship and endogenous growth," *Center for Economic Policy Research*, London, UK, December No. 4783

Acs, Z. and, D. Evans, (1994). "The Determinants of Variations in Self-employment Rates across Countries and Over time", working paper.

Acs, Z. and C. Armington. (2003). "Job Creation and Persistence in Services and Manufacturing," *The Papers on Entrepreneurship, Growth, and Public Policy*, No. 1604.

Acs, Z., C. Armington, and T. Zhang, (2007). "The Determinants of New Firm Survival in Regional Economies: the Role of Regional Human Capital Stock and Knowledge Spillovers," *Papers in Regional Science*, vol. 86, issue 3.

Anderson, A.R. (2000). Paradox in the periphery: an entrepreneurial reconstruction? *Entrepreneurship & Regional Development,* Vol.12, issue 2. p.91-19

Anselin L, Varga A, Acs Z (1997) "Local geographic spillovers between university research and high-technology innovation," *Journal of Urban Economics* 42: 422–448

Anselin L, Varga A, Acs Z (2000) "Geographic and sectoral characteristics of academic knowledge externalities," *Papers in Regional Science* 79(4): 435–443

Armington C, Acs Z (2002) The determinants of regional variation in firm formation. *Regional Studies* 36(1): 33–45

Arrow, K. (1962). "The Economic Implications of Learning by Doing." *Review of Economic Studies* 29, no. 3: 155 - 173.

Atchley, R.C. (1972). *The Social Forces in Later Life*. Belmont, CA: Wadsworth.

Atkinson R. D. and R. H. Court (1998). *The "new economy" Index: Understanding America's Economic Transformation*. Washington, DC: Progress. Policy Inst.

Atkinson, R.D., Court, R. H., and Ward, J. M. (1999). *THE STATE NEW ECONOMY INDEX: Benchmarking Economic Transformation in the States.* Progressive Policy Institute Technology & New Economy Project. Retrieved on Dec 3, 3004 from World Wide Web http://www.neweconomyindex.org/states/1999/StateNewEcon.pdf.

Audretsch, D.B. and M. Keilbach (2004). "Entrepreneurial Capital and Economic Performance., discussion paper. *Entrepreneurship, Growth and Public Policy.* Jena, Germany: Max Plank Institute.

Audretsch, D.B. and A.R. Thurik (2001). Linking Entrepreneurship to Growth, STI Working Paper 2001/2, Paris: OECD.

Autio, E. and Leskelä, R. (2001). Research and Technological Development and Entrepreneurial Activity: A Closer Look. *Global Entrepreneurship Monitor (GEM): 2001 Executive Report.* Kansas City, MO: Ewing Marion Kauffman Foundation, Kauffman Center for Entrepreneurial Leadership

Ayer, R. (n.d.). Older Workers Make A Difference. The Hartford Financial Services Group.

Bailey, N. and Turok, I. (2001) 'Central Scotland as a polycentric urban region: useful planning concept or chimera?', *Urban Studies*, 38, 697-715.

Barnett, D. (2000). History of Entrepreneurship Theory. *Technopreneurial.com.* [Online]. Available: http://www.technopreneurial.com/articles/references.asp [2002, June 20]

Barro, Robert J. and Jong-Wha Lee (1994), "Sources of Economic Growth (with comments from Nancy Stokey)" *Carnegie-Rochester Conference Series on Public Policy* 40: 1-57.

Barro, R. J. and X. Sala-i-Martin. (1992) "Convergence," *Journal of Political Economy* 100: 223-51.

Barro, R. J. and X. Sala-i-Martin (1995), *Economic Growth*, New York; London and Montreal: McGraw-Hill.

Barth, M.C., McNaught, W., and Rizzi, P.(1993). "Corporations and the aging labor force," in P.H. Mirvis (ed.), *Building the Competitive Labor force: Investing in Human Capital for Corporate Success,* New York: John Wiley & Sons.

Battelle et al. (2000). Advanced Traveler Information Services in Rural Tourism Areas: Branson Travel and Recreation Information Program (Missouri) and Interstate Traveler and Tourist Information System (Arizona). Department of Transportation.

Baumol W. J. (1993). "Formal entrepreneurship theory in economics: existence and bounds," *Journal of Business Venturing*, 3.

Baumol, W. J. (2002). "The Free-Market Innovation Machine: Analysing the Growth Miracle of Capitalism," Princeton University Press.

Becker, G. S., K. M. Murphy, and R. Tamura. (1990) "Human Capital, Fertility, and Economic Growth," *Journal of Political Economy 98:* S12 - 37.

Becker, G. S. (1992). "The Economic Way of Looking At Life." Nobel Lecture, December 9, 1992.

Becker, G. S. (1993). *Human Capital: A Theoretical and Empirical Analysis with Special Reference to Education.* (3rd edition). Chicago, USA and London, UK: The University of Chicago Press.

Bengtson, V. L. (1969). "Cultural and Occupational Differences in Level of Present Role Activity in Retirement." In R. J. Havighurst, J. M. A. Municks, B. C. Neugarten, and H, Thomas (Eds.), *Adjustments to Retirement: A Cross-national Study.* Assen, The Netherlands: Van Gorkum.

Bengtson, V. L., E. O. Burgess, and T. M. Parrott. (1997). "Theory, Explanation and a Third Generation of Theoretical Development in Social Gerontology." *Journal of Gerontology,* 1997, 52B, S72-S88.

Benz, M. and Frey, B.S. (2004). "Being independent raises happiness at work" *Swedish Economic Policy Review* 11 (2004) 95-134.

Berkovec, J. and Stern, S., (1991). "Job Exit Behavior of Older Men," *Econometrica,* Vol. 59, No. 1 (Jan 1991), p. 189-210.

Blanchflower, D.G. and Oswald, A.J. (1990). "Self-employment and the Enterprise Culture". In Jowell, R., Witherspoon, S., Jowell, R (Eds.), *British Social Attitudes: The 1990 Report.* Gower Press, Aldershot.

Blanchflower, D.G. and Oswald, A.J. (1998). "What Makes An Entrepreneur?" *Journal of Labor Economics Perspectives,* issue 9, p. 153-167, Summer.

Blanchflower, D.G., (2000). "Self-employment in OECD Countries." *Labour Economics,* Issue 7, p.471-505.

Blanchflower, D.G., Oswald, A.J., and Stutzer, A., (2001). "Latent entrepreneurship across nations," *European Economic Review* 45, p. 680-691.

Blau, D., (1987). " A Time-series Analysis of Self-employment in the United States." *Journal of Political Economy,* issue 95, p. 445-467.

Blau, D., (1994). "Labor Force Dynamics of Older Men," *Econometrica,* Vol. 62, No.1 (Jan 1994), p. 117-156.

Blöndal, S. and Scarpetta, S. (1999). "The Retirement Decision in OECD Countries." *OECD Economics Department Working Papers*, No. 202. Paris: Organization for Economic Cooperation and Development. http://www.oecd.org/dataoecd/36/30/1866098.pdf.

Board of Trustees of the Federal Old-Age and Survivors Insurance and Disability Insurance Trust Funds. (2000). *2000 Annual Report*. Washington DC: Social Security Administration.

Bogenhold, D. and Staber, U., (1991). "The Decline and Rise of Self-employment." *Employment and Society*, issue 5, p. 223-239.

Booz Allen & Hamilton Inc. (1994). Evaluation of Phase II of the *SmarTraveler* Advanced Traveler Information System Operational Test. Cambridge, MA: Multisystems.

Brown, S. K. (2003). "Staying Ahead of the Curve 2003:The AARP Working in Retirement Study." *AARP Knowledge Management*: Washington DC.

Bruce, D., Holtz-Eakin, D., and Quinn, J. (2000). "Self-employment and Labor Market Transitions at Older Ages". *Center for Retirement Research at Boston College Working Paper* 2000-13. Chestnut Hill, MA: Center for Retirement Research at Boston College.

Burke, A. E. and Fitzroy, F. R. (2006). "Education and Regional Job Creation by the Self-employed: The English North-South Divide," *The Papers on Entrepreneurship, Growth, and Public Policy*, No. 0706.

Burtless, G. and Quinn, J.F.. (2000). "Retirement Trends and Policies to Encourage Work among Older Americans." In Allan Hunt (ed.), *Ensuring Health and Income Security for an Aging Labor force*. Kalamazoo, MI: W.E. Upjohn Institute for Employment Research.

Callaban, D. (2000). "Heath Care Struggle Between Young and Old." E. W. Markson & L. A. Hollis-Sawyer (Eds.). *Intersections of aging: Readings in social gerontology*. Los Angeles: Roxbury.

Cantillon, Richard. (1755). *Essai sur la nature de commerce en géneral*. Henry Higgs. Ed. London: Macmillan, 1931.

Carrasco, R. and Ejrnas, M. (2003). "Self-employment In Denmark and Spain" Institutions, Economic Conditions, an Gender Differences". Universidad Carlos III de Madrid, Mimeo.

Charness, N.. (2004). "The Age-Ability-Productivity Paradox". Conference processing of a Wharton Impact Conference, *Maximizing Your Labor force: Employees Over 50 In Today's Global Economy*. Nov. 10, 2004. University of Pennsylvania and AARP Global Aging Program.

Christaller, L.W. (1933). *Die zentralen Orte in Südeutschland*. Jena: Fischer.

CIA World Fact Book (2005). Retrieved from World Wide Web http://www.cia.gov/cia/publications/factbook/geos/U.S..html..

Ciccone, A. and Hall, R. E. (1996), "Productivity and the density of economic activity", *American Economic Review*, 86(1), p.54-70, 1996.

Clark, R. L., York, E. A., and Anker, R.. (1999). "Economic development and labor force participation of older persons." *Population Research and Policy Review* 18: 411–432.

Clemons, J.,et al. (1999). ARTIMIS Telephone Travel Information Service Current Use Patterns and User Satisfaction. Kentucky, Ohio: Kentucky Transportation Center, University of Kentucky.

Collison, J. (program manager). (2003). "Older Workers Survey." SHRM research, June 2003. Society for Human Resource Management (SHRM), National Older Worker Career Center (NOWCC) and Committee for Economic Development (CED).

Committee for Economic Development, 1999 "New Opportunities For Older Workers", Committee for Economic Development, 1999 (from Fuller, print out copy]

Copus, A. K. (2001). From Core-periphery to Polycentric Development Concepts of Spatial and Aspatial Peripherality. *European Planning Studies*, Vol. 9, No. 4. New York, USA: Taylor & Francis.

Cottrell, L. (1942). "The Adjustment of the Individual to His Age and Sex Roles". American Sociological Review, 1942, 7, p. 617-620.

Covey, H. (1981). "A reconceptualization of Continuity Theory: Some Preliminary Thoughts." The Gerontologists, 1981-21, p. 628-633.

Crown, W. H. and Longino, C. F., Jr. (2000). "Labor Force Trends and Aging Policy." E. W. Markson & L. A. Hollis-Sawyer (Eds.). *Intersections of aging: Readings in social gerontology*. Los Angeles: Roxbury.

Dalen, H.P. van and K. Henkens. (2002). "Early retirement reform. Can it and will it work?" Ageing and Society 22(2): 209–231.

Day, C and S. Dowrick. (2004). "Aging Economics: Human Capital, Productivity and Fertility." Agenda 2004, vol. 11, issue 1, pp. 1-20.

Department of Transportation. (1997). Improving Transportation for a Maturing Society. Office of the Assistant Secretary for Transportation Policy: DOT-P10-97-01.

Department of Transportation. (2002). New 511 Traveler Information System: Summary Information. Retrieved December 2003 from World Wide Web: http://doroads/nol/org/roadrunner/docs/archieves/rr-dec-jan01-2.pdf.

Department of Transportation. (2003). Internet and Telephone Traveler Information Systems Influence Commuter Behavior More Effectively than Radio/TV Broadcasts. Retrieved December 2003 from World Wide Web: http://www.benefitcost.its.dot.gov/ITS/benecost.nsf/ByLink/BOTM-December2003.

Doeringer, P.B. (ed.) (1990). *Bridges to Retirement: Older Workers in a Changing Labor Market*. Ithaca, New York: ILR press. Pp. x, 237.

Domencich, T. and D. McFadden. 1975. *Urban Travel Demand*. Amsterdam: North Holland Publishing Company.

Dunne, E. (1990). The Learning Society: International Perspectives on Core Skills in Higher Education. London: Kogan Page.

Duval, R. (2003). Retirement behaviour in OECD countries: impact of old-age pension schemes and other social transfer programmes. *OECD Economic Studies* Summer 2003 i37 p5(45).

Estes, C. L., and Associates (2000). *Social Policy and Aging: A Critical Perspective*. Thousand Oaks: sage.

European Spatial Planning Observation Network (ESPON) (2003). The Role, Specific Situation and Potentials of Urban Areas As Nodes in a Polycentric Development. *ESPON Project*. 1.1.1. Second interim report. Stockholm, Sweden.

Evans, D. and Jovanovic, B. (1989). "An Empirical Analysis of Self-employment in the Netherlands". *Economics Letters*, issue 32, p. 97-100.

Evans, D. and B. Jovanovic. 1989. "An Estimated Model of Entrepreneurial Liquidity Constraints," *Journal of Political Economy* 97: 808-827.

Evans and Leighton (1989). "Some Empirical Aspects of Entrepreneurship". *American Economic Review*, issue 79, p 519-535.

Everitt, B. S., and G. Dunn, G. (1991). *Applied multivariate data analysis*. London: Edward Arnold.

Faludi, A. (2004). The European Spatial Development Perspective and North-west Europe: Application and the Future. *European Planning Studies*,Vol.12,No.3,April 2004. Taylor & Francis Group: carfax publishing

Fairfax County Economic Development Authority. (2004). "History of Fairfax County, Virginia". Website of *Visit Fairfax*. Retrieved on Nov 29, 2004 from world wide web http://www.visitfairfax.org/history.php.

Federal Highway Administration. (1998). Older Driver Highway Design Handbook: recommendations and Guidelines. Retrieved October 2003 from World Wide Web: http://safety.fhwa.dot.gov/programs/olderdriver.htm.

Felsenstein, D. and A. Fleischer. (2002). Small-Scale Entrepreneurhsip and Acess to Capital in Peripheral Locations: An Empirical Analysis. *Growth and Change*, Vol. 33 (Spring 2002), p. 196- 215.

Florida, R. (2004). *The rise of the creative class : and how it's transforming work, leisure, community and everyday life.* New York, NY : Basic Books.

Florida, R. (2005). *The Flight of Creative Class: The New Global Competition for Talent.* New York , NY: Harper Business.

Foray, D. and B.D. Lundyall. (1996). "The "knowledge-based economy". From the Economics of Knowledge to the Learning Economy." In *Employment and Growth in the "knowledge-based economy".* Paris: OECD, pp. 11-32.

Friedberg, L.. (2003). "The Impact Of Technological Change On Older Workers: Evidence From Data On Computer Use," Industrial and Labor Relations Review, v56 (3, Apr), 511- 529.

Fuchs, V. (1982). "Self-employment and Labor Force Participation on Elder Males". *Journal of Human Resources*, issue 17, p.339-357.

Garofalo, G. A. and Yamarik, S. (2002). Regional Convergence: Evidence from a New State-by-state Capital Stock Series. *The Review of Economics and Statistics,* May 2002, 84(2): 316–323. The President and Fellows of Harvard College and the Massachusetts Institute of Technology

Garreau, J. (1991), Edge City: Life on the New Frontier, New York, NY: Doubleday.

Gendell, M.. (2001). "Retirement age declines again in 1990s." *Monthly Labor Review* October 2001. http://www.bls.gov/opub/mlr/2001/10/art2full.pdf.

Getis, A. and J. Getis (1970). "Christaller's Central Place Theory". F. Dohrs and L. Sommers. (Eds). *Economic Geography: Selected Readings.* Thomas Y. Crowell, Inc.

Giannetti, M. and Simonov, A. (2004). "On the determinants of Entrepreneurial activity: Social norms, economic environment and individual Characteristics," *Swedish Economic Policy Review* 11 (2004) 269-313.

Gilroy, R., Puentes, R. & Schuman, R.. (Ed.) (1998). Choosing the Route to Traveler Information Systems Deployment: Decision Factors for Creating Public-Private Business Plans, an Action Guide. U.S. Department of Transportation: Intelligent Transportation Society of America.

Glaeser EL, Kallal HD, Scheinkman JA, Shleifer A (1992) Growth in cities. *Journal of Political Economy* 100:1126-1152.

Glaeser, E., Scheinkman, J. & Shleifer, A. (1995). "Economic Growth in a Cross-Section of Cities", *Journal of Monetary Economics*, 36: 117-143.

Global Entrepreneurship Monitor, (2001). *Global Entrepreneurship Monitor 2004 Executive Report*. P. D. Reynolds, S. M. Camp, W. D. Bygrave, E. Autio, M. Hay (GEM Research Committee), Babson College, IBM, London Business School, and the Kauffman Center for Entrepreneurial Leadership.

Global Entrepreneurship Monitor, (2004). *Global Entrepreneurship Monitor 2004 Executive Report*. Z. J. Acs, P. Arenims, M. Hay, M. Minniti (GEM Research Committee), Babson College and London Business School.

Greenspan, A. (1999). "The Interaction of Education and Economic Change." Federal Reserve Bank of Minneapolis. 13 (1): 6-11.

Greenspan, A.. (2004). Opening remarks at a symposium sponsored by the Federal Reserve Bank of Kansas City, Jackson Hole, Wyoming . August 27, 2004. Retrieved from the World Wide Web on October 27, 2005 at http://www.seniorjournal.com/NEWS/Money/4-08-27Greenspan.htm.

Gore, C. (1984). Regions in Question: Space, Development Theory and Regional Policy. London: Menthuen

Grossman, G. M. and Helpman, E., 1991, "Endogenous Product Cycles," *The Economic Journal* 101: 1214 - 1229

Grossman, G. M. and Helpman, E., (1994), "Endogenous Innovation in the Theory of Growth," *Journal of Economic Perspectives* 8: 23 – 44.

Guillemar, A., P. Taylor, and Walker, A.. (1996). "Managing an ageing labor force in Britain and France," *The Geneva Papers on Risk and Insurance* 21: 478-501.

Hagen, E. (1962). *On the Theory of Economic Change: How Economic Growth Begins*, Homewood, Illinois: Dorsey.

Hagestad, G., and B. Neugarten (1985). "Age and the Life Course". In R.H. Binstock and E. Shanas 9Eds.), *Handbook of Aging and the Social Sciences* (2nd ed.). New York: Van Nostrand.

Hamilton, B. H. (2000). "Does Entrepreneurship Pay? An Empirical Analysis of the Return to Self-employment". *Journal of Political Economy*, Issue 108, p. 604-631.

Hart, D.M. (2003). *The Emergency of Entrepreneurship Policy: Governance, Start-ups, and Growth in the U.S. "Knowledge Economy"*. New York, U.S.: Cambridge.

Hayflick, L. (1980). "The Cell biology of Human Aging." *Scientific American*. 1980, 242, P. 60.

Haub, C. (2003)."The U.S. Birth Rate Falls Further." Population Research Bureau: http://www.prb.org/Template.cfm?Section=PRB&template=/ContentManagement/ContentDisplay.cfm&ContentID=8838.

Henk, R. & Kuhn, B. T. (2000). Assessing The Effectiveness of Advanced Traveler Information On Older Driver Traveler Behavior and Mode Choice. College Station, Texas: Texas Transportation Institute at the Texas A & M University System.

Henkens, K.. (2000). "Supervisors' attitudes about early retirement of subordinates," *Journal of Applied Social Psychology* 30(4): 833–852.

Herman, R., Olivio, T. and Gioia, J. (2003). *Impending Crisis: Too Many Jobs, Too Few People*. Winchester, VA: Oakhill Press

Higgins, B. and D. J. Savoie (1995). *Regional development Theories and Their Application*. New Jersey: New Brunswick.

High, J. (2004). "The roles of entrepreneurship in economic growth", in: H.L.F.P.

Hirschman, A.O. (1958). *The Strategy of Economic Development*. New Haven, CT: Yale University Press.

Holtz-Eakin, D., D. Joulfaian, and H. S. Rosen. 1994a. "Entrepreneurial Decisions and Liquidity Constraints," *Rand Journal of Economics* 25(2) (Summer): 334-347.

Holtz-Eakin, D., D. Joulfaian, and H. S. Rosen. 1994b. "Sticking it Out: Entrepreneurial Survival and Liquidity Constraints," *Journal of Political Economy* 102 (February): 53-75

Hooymann, N. R. and Kiyak, H. A.. (2005). *Social Gerontology: A multidisciplinary Perspective*. Boston: Allyn and Bacon. Chapter 1, 8, 9, 12, 14, 16.

Human Resources Development Canada, (1999). "Older Worker Adjustment Programs Lessons Learned (Final Report): Evaluation and Data Development Strategic Policy." Human Resources Development Canada, Government of Canada: SP-AH093-12-99E. Retrieved from World Wide Web on Aug 30, 2005 at http://www11.hrdcdrhc.gc.ca/pls/edd/OWAP_134000.htm.

Ippolito, R. A.. (1990). "Toward Explaining Earlier Retirement After 1970." *Industrial & Labor Relations Review*. July 1990. Vol. 43, No. 5. P. 556. Cornell University.

190

Jarboe, K. P. and Alliance, A. (2001). "Knowledge Management As an Economic Development Strategy." *Reviews of Economic Development Literature and Practice*: No.7. Economic Development Administration, U.S. Department of Commerce.

Jacobs, J. (1969), *The economy of cities*. New York: Vintage.

Jarboe, K. P. and Alliance, A. (2001). Knowledge Management As an Economic Development Strategy. *Reviews of Economic Development Literature and Practice*: No.7. Economic Development Administration, U.S. Department of Commerce.

Jaffe A, Tratjenberg M, Henderson R (1993) "Geography, location of knowledge spillovers as evidence of patent citations," *Quarterly Journal of Economics* 108: 483–499.

Jarboe, K. P. and Alliance, A., 2001. "Knowledge Management As an Economic Development Strategy." *Reviews of Economic Development Literature and Practice*: No.7. Economic Development Administration, U.S. Department of Commerce.

Jin, D. and R.R. Stough (1998) "Learning and Learning Capabilities in the Fordist and Post-Fordist Age: An Integrative Framework." *Environment & Planning*. A 30: 1255-1278.

Johansson, Mats. (2002). "Polycentric Urban Structures in Sweden – Conditions and Prospects". Bengs, Christer (Ed). *Facing ESPON*.. Stockholm. *Nordregio Report* 2002:1.

Johnson, R. (2001). "Why the 'average age of retirement' is a misleading measure of labor supply." *Monthly Labor Review*. December 2001. http://www.bls.gov/opub/mlr/2001/12/comntry.pdf.

Johnson, W. (1978). "A Theory of Job-Shopping" *Quarterly Journal of Economics*, May 1978, issue 22, p. 261-78.

Karoly, L. A. and J. Zissimopoulos (2004). "Self-employment and The 50+ Population." *AARP*, #2004-03.

King, L. J. (1985). *Central Place Theory*. Beverly Hills, CA: Sage.

Kirzner, I.M.. (1973). *Competition & Entrepreneurship*. Chicago: University of Chicago Press.

Kirzner, I.M. (1997), Entrepreneurial Discovery and The Competitive Market Process: An Austrian Approach, *Journal of Economic Literature* 35, 60-85.Lucas, R. E., Jr., (1988) "On the Mechanics of Economic Development," *Journal of Monetary Economics 22: 3-42.*

Kline, Rex B. (1998). *Principles and practice of structural equation modeling*. NY: Guilford Press. A very readable introduction to the subject, with good coverage of assumptions and SEM's relation to underlying regression, factor, and other techniques.

Lang, R. (2003). *Edgeless Cities*. Washington, Brookings Press.

Lazear, E.P. (1998), *Personnel Economics for Managers*, New York: Wiley.

Lazear, E. (2002), 'Entrepreneurship", *NBER Working Paper* 9109, National Bureau of Economic Research, Cambridge, MA.Long, J.E. (1982). "The Income Tax and Self-employment." *National Tax Journal*, issue 35, p. 31-42, March.

Lipton, M. (1977) *Why Poor People Stay Poor: Urban Bias in World Development*. Cambridge, Mass.: Harvard University Press.

Litwak, E and Longino, C.F. (no date). Migration Pattern among the Elderly: A Developmental. Retrieved January 2004 from World Wide Web: http://www.usc.edu/dept/gero/AgeWorks/gero530/week5/pages/week5-read-text.PDF.

Lordkipanidze, M. (2002). Enhancing Entrepreneurship in Rural Tourism for Sustainable Regional Development: The case of Söderslätt region, Sweden. *IIIEE Reports*, 2002:10. Lund, Sweden: IIIEE.

Low, S., J. Henderson, and S. Weiler (2005). "Gauging a Region's Entrepreneurial Potential," Federal Reserve Bank of Kansas City- Economic Review, 3rd quarter, 2005.

Lösch, A. (1940). *Die räumliche Ordung der Wirtschaft*. Jena: Fischer. Translated by W.H. Woglom and W.F. Stolper (1954). *The Economics of Location*. New Heaven, CT: Yale University Press.

Lucas, R. E., (1988), "On the mechanics of economic development," Journal of Monetary *Economics* 22: 3 - 42.

Lundvall, B.and B. Johnson. (1994), *The Learning Economy*. Journal of Industry Studies 1(2), pp. 23-42.

Malizia, E. E. (1986). "Economic Development in Smaller Cities and Rural Areas". *Planner's Notebook*. Autumn 1986.

Mankiw, N. G. (2005). "Macroeconomics." (5th ed.). New York: Worth Publishers.

Mankiw, N. G., D. Romer, and D. N. Weil, (1992). "A Contribution to the Empirics of Economic Growth," *Quarterly Journal of Economics*, May 1992, 107 (2), 407–37.

Marshall, A (1930). *Principles of economics*. London: Macmillan and Co.

Marshall, V. W. (1994). "Sociology and Psychology in the Theoretical Legacy of the Kansas City studies." *The Gerontologist,* 1994, 34, p. 768-774.

Mason, C. (1991). Spatial variations in enterprise: the geography of new firm foundation, in Burrows, R. (ed.) *Deciphering the Enterprise Culture*. London: Routledge.

McClelland, D. (1961). *The Achieving Society*, New Jersey: Van Nostrand.

Meager, N.. (1992). "Does Unemployment Lead to Self-employment?" *Small Business Economics*, issue 4, p. 87-103.

Meyer, J.R. (1968). "Regional Economics: A Survey." *American Econ. Review*, vol.53, 1963, pp.19-54. (reprinted in Needleman, L. ed., Regional Economics, 1968, pp.19ff.)

Miller, R. (1984) "Job Matching and Occupational Choice," *Journal of Political Economy*. December 1984, issue 92, p. 1086-120.

Minkler, M. and C. Estes (1984). *Readings in the Political Economy of Aging*. Farmingdale, NY: Baywood.

Mincer, J. (1974) *Schooling, Experience, and Earnings* (New York: Columbia University Press for the National Bureau of Economic Research).

Murphy, K. M. and Welch, F. (1992) "The Structure of Wages," *Quarterly Journal of Economics* 107: 285 - 326.

Myrdal, G. (1957). *Economic Theory and Underdeveloped Regions*. London: Duckworth.

Nahuis, R.(2003). *Knowledge, Inequality and Growth in The New Economy*. Northampton, MA: Edward Elgar.

National Commission on Entrepreneurship (NCOE) (2004), Fact Sheet, http://www.publicforuminstitute.org/nde/news/facts.htm.

National Household Travel Survey Pre- and Post-9/11 Data. Retrieved from the World Wide web http://www.bts.gov/programs/national_household_travel_survey/pre_and_post_9_11_dat a_documentation/index.html.

Nelson, A. (1993). "Theories of Regional Development" in *Theories of Local Economic Development*. R. Bingham and R. Mier, eds, Sage. Pp. 27-29.

Nelson, A. C. (1999). "Comparing States With and Without Growth Management: Analysis Based on Indicators With Policy Implications." *Land Use Policy* 16: 121-127.Neugarten, B., R. J. Havighurst, and S. S. Tobin (1968). "Personality and Patterns of Aging." In B. L. Neugarten (Ed.), *Middle Age and Aging*. Chicago: University of Chicago Press.

Nijkamp, P. and J. Poot. (1993). Endogenous Technological Change, Innovation Diffusion and Transitional Dynamics in a Nonlinear Growth Model. *Australian Economic Papers*: Vol 32, issue 61, p. 191-161.

Olson, L. K. (1982). *The Political Economy of Aging*. New York: Columbia University Press.

Orski, K.. (No date). Broadcasting vs. "Narrowcasting" of Traveler Information: Competing Service Delivery Models Will Be Tested in the Washington Metropolitan Area. Retrieved October 2003 from World Wide Web: http://www.itsonline.com/ko_ncast.html.

Overbo, B. and M. Minkler (1993). "The Lives of Older Women: Perspectives from Political Economy and the Humanities." In T. R. Cole, W. A. Achenbaum, P. L. Jakobi, and R. Kastenbaum (Ed.), *Voices and Visions of Aging: Toward a Critical Gerontology*. New York: Springer.

Parker, S. C. and Rougaier, J. (2004). "The Retirement Behaviour of the Self-employed in Britain". University of Durham, *working paper in Economics and Finance*, No. 04/08.

Pawlovich, M. D. (2002) Iowa Highway Safety Management System. http://www.iowasms.org/toolbox.htm. Chapter 7 Sustaining Safe Mobility in Older Drivers. http://www.iowasms.org/pdfs/toolbox/chapter08.pdf.Chapter 20 accommodating Older Drivers.

Perroux, F (1955) "Note sur la notion de pole de croissance", *Economie Appliquee*, 8, p307-320. or in I. Livingstone (1979) *Development Economics and Policy: Selected Readings*. London: George Allen & Unwin.

Peterson, P. G., 1999. *Gray Dawn: How the Coming Age Wave Will Transform America—and the World*. Times Books, Random House: New York.

Picot, G. and Manser, M.. (1999). "The role of self-employment in job creation in Canada and the United States". *Canadian Economic Observer*, v.12(3) Mr'99 pg 3.1-3.17.

Piazza-Georgi, B. (2002). The Role of Human and Social Capital in Growth: Extending Our Understanding. *Cambridge Journal of Economics*. Vol. 26, issue 4, p. 461-479.

Polachek, S.W. & W.S. Siebert (1993), *The Economics of Earnings*, Cambridge, MA: Cambridge University Press. Mertens, N. (1998), *Loopbaanonderbrekingen en kinderen: gevolgen voor de beloning van vrouwen*, PhD thesis, Utrecht University.

Psacharopoulos, G. (1975) *Earnings and Education in OECD Countries* (Paris: Organization for Economic Co-operation; Washington, D.C.: OECD Publications Center).

Putnam, R. D. 1995. "Bowling Alone: America's Declining Social Capital," *The Journal of Democracy,* (6)1, 65-78.

Quinn, J.F. (1980). "Labor-force Participation Patterns of Older Self-employed Workers". *Social Security Bulletin*, 43(4), p. 17-28.

Ray, R.E. (1996). "A Post Modern Perspective on Feminist Gerontology." *The Gerontologist*, 1996, 36, p. 674-680.

Reardon, E. (1997). "Self-employment in Canada and the United States." Unpublished paper, June 1997.

Reich, R., (1992). *The Work of Nations*. New York: Vintage Books.

Remery, C., Henkens, K., Schippers, J., and Ekamper, P. (2003). "Managing an aging labor force and a tight labor market: views held by Dutch employers." *Population Research and Policy Review* 22: 21–40, 2003. Kluwer Academic Publishers. The Netherlands.

Resnick, B., Mills, M. E., and Nahm, E. (2004). "Web Use Can Improve Quality of Life for Elders," *Maximizing Human Potential*, Vol. 11, No. 3 (Winter 2004). pp. 4, 6.

Reynolds, P. D. et al., 2005, 'Global Entrepreneurship Monitor: Data Collection Design and Implementation 1998-2003', *Small Business Economics* **24**, 205-231.

Rix, S. E. (2004). "Aging and Work—A View From The United States." AARP Public Policy Institute: #2004-02.

Romer, P. M., (1986), "Increasing returns and long-run growth," *Journal of Political Economy* 94: 1002 - 1037.

Romer, P. M., (1990) "Endogenous Technological Change." *Journal of Political Economy* 98(5), pp. 71-102

Romer, P. M. (1993). "Implementing a National Technology Strategy with Self-Organizing Industry Investment Boards." Brookings Papers on Economic Activity: Microeconomics 2: 345.

Romer, P. M. (1994). "New goods, old theory and the welfare costs of trade restrictions." *Journal of Development Economics* 43: 5.

RoperASW, (2002). "Staying Ahead of the Curve: The AARP Work and Career Study." AARP: Washington DC.

Rural Development Council. (2001). Entrepreneurship in rural America. *Culture & Entrepreneurship*. [Online]. Available: http://www.wvrdc.state.wv.U.S./chapter3.pdf [2002, July 29]

Saxenian, A.L. (1994) *Regional Advantage: Culture and Competition in Silicon Valley and Route 128* Cambridge, MA: Harvard University Press.

Say, J.B. (1845). *A Treatise On Political Economy*. 4th ed., translated by C.R.Prinsep. Philadelphia: Grigg & Elliot.

Schetagne, S.. (2001). Building Bridges *Across Generations in the Workplace: A Response to Aging of the Labor force.* Vancouver, Canada: Columbia Foundation.

195

Schuetze, H. J. (2000). "Taxes, Economic Conditions and Recent Trends in Self-employment: A Canada-U.S. Comparison", *Labour Economics*, issue 7, p. 507-554.

Schuetze, H. J. and Bruce, D. (2004). "Tax policy and entrepreneurship," *Swedish Economic Policy Review* 11 (2004) 233-265.

Schultz, T. W.. (1963) *The Economic Value of Education* (New York: Columbia University Press).

Schulz, R. and T. A. Salthouse. (1999). *Adult development and aging: Myths and emerging realities* (3rd Edition). Upper Saddle River, New Jersey: Prentice Hall.

Schumpeter, J. (1950) *Capitalism, Socialism, and Democracy*, 3rd edition, Harper and Row, New York, 1950.

Schumpeter, J.A. (1961). *The Theory of Economic Development* (2 nd ed.). New York: Oxford University Press.

Shane, S. (2000), Prior knowledge and the discovery of entrepreneurial opportunities, *Organization Science* 11, 448-469.

Skinner, D. & Stearns, M. D. (1999). Safe Mobility in an Aging World. Washington, D.C.: Annual Meeting of the Transportation Research Board.

Smith, L. (2006), "How we age is becoming a growing curriculum," Batimore Sun, December 31, 2006. Retrieved from the World Wide Web http://www.baltimoresun.com/features/custom/modernlife/bal-ml.boomer31dec31,0,3717492.story.

Social Security Administration, (1999). "Social Security Bulletin, Annual Statistical Supplement," Bureau of Labor Statistics publications and Web site. See Murray Gendell and Jacob S. Siegel, "Trends in retirement age by sex, 1950–2005," *Monthly Labor Review*, July 1992, pp. 22– 29, for more information about the labor force data.

Social Security Advisory Board. (1999). *Forum on Implications of Raising the Social Security Retirement Age*. Washington, DC: Social Security Advisory Board, May.

Social Security Administration. (2004). *Overview of SSA: SSA's FY 2004 Performance and Accountability Report*. Retrieved on the World Wide Web at http://www.ssa.gov/finance/2004/Overview.pdf.

Sokolovsky, J., (2000). "Images of Aging," E. W. Markson & L. A. Hollis-Sawyer (Eds.). *Intersections of aging: Readings in social gerontology*. Los Angeles: Roxbury.

Solow, R. S. (1957). "Technical Change and the Aggregate Production Function." *Review of Economics and Statistics* 39: 312-20.

196

Soolman, J and Radin, S.. (2000). Features of Traffic and Transit Internet Sites. Volpe National Transportation Systems, Department of Transportation.

Sterns, H. L. and McDaniel, M. A. (1994). "Job Performance and the Older Worker." In Sara E. Rix (Editor), *Older Workers: How Do They Measure Up?* Washington, DC: AARP.

Steuerle, C. E. (2005). "SOCIAL SECURITY—A LABOR FORCE ISSUE," Statement before the Subcommittee on Social Security Committee on Ways and Means United States House of Representatives, June 14, 2005.

Stohr, W. B. and F. Todtling. (1977) "An evaluation of regional policies experiences in market and mixed economies." in N. M. Hansen (Ed.) (1978) *Human Settlement Systems: International Perspectives on Structure, Change and Public Policy.* Cambridge, Mass.: Ballinger.

Stolarick, K. M, (n.d.) "Social Tolerance Index", [data series] 2000 metropolitan area statistics, 2005 (personal communication).

Stough, R. R. and Kulkarni, R. (2004). Cities and Business. *Urban Dynamics and Growth, CEA,* vol. 266. P. 659-9687. Amsterdam: Elsevier B.V.

Suarez-Villa, L. (2004). Technocapitalism and The New Ecology of Entrepreneurship. De Groot, H. L. F., et al. (Ed.). *Entrepreneurship and Regional Economic Development: A Spatial Perspective.* Northampton, MA, USA: Edward Elgar.

Taylor, M. P., (1996). "Earnings, Independence or Unemployment: Why Become Self-employed?" *Oxford Bulletin of Economics and Statistics*, issue 58 (2), p. 253-265.

Taylor, M. P., (1997). "The Changing Picture of Self-employment in Britain," *Institute for Social and Economic Research (ISER) working papers*, 1997-09.

Taylor, P. and Walker, A.. (1998). "Employers and older workers: attitudes and employment practices," *Ageing and Society* 18(6): 641–658.

Thurow, L.C. (1975). *Generating Inequality*, New York: Basic Books.

Toppen, A., et al. (2002). Time Management Benefits of ATIS for Unfamiliar Urban_Drivers. Washington D.C.: the 9th World Congress Conference.

Treas, J.. (1995). Older Americans in the 1990's and Beyond, *Population Bulletin*, Vol. 50, No.2. Washington, DC: Population Reference Bureau, Inc..

U.S. Administration on Aging. (2002). *A Profile of Older Americans.* Washington, DC.

U.S. census Bureau. (2001). *The 65 Years and Over Population: 2000.* C2KBR/01-10. Washington, DC: October 2001.

U.S. Census Bureau. (2000). Population Estimates and American Community Survey. http://factfinder.census.gov/.

U.S. Department of Labor, Bureau of Labor Statistics,(1994-2005). http://data.bls.gov/PDQ/servlet/SurveyOutputServlet.

Van der Sluis, J. and van Praag, C. M., (2004). "Economic returns to education for entrepreneurs: The development of a neglected child in the family of economics of education?" *Swedish Economic Policy Review* 11 (2), 2004.

Van Praag, C. M. (1999). Some classic views on entrepreneurship. *Journal DE Economist* 147, No 3, 311- 335, Kluwer Academic Publishers.

Van Stel A. J. and D. J. Storey (2004). "The Link between Firm Birth and Job Creation: Is There a Upas Tree Effect?" *The Papers on Entrepreneurship, Growth, and Public Policy*, No. 3304.

Wagner, D.L.. (1998), *Factors Influencing the Use of Older Workers: A Survey of U.S. Employers*, Washington, DC: The National Council on the Aging.

Waldman, D. A. and B. J. Avolio (1986). "A Meta-Analysis of Age Differences in Job Performance." *Journal of Applied Psychology*, No. 71, pp. 33-38.

Warntz, W. (1967). Global science and the tyranny of space, *Papers and Proceedings of the Regional Science Association*, issue19, p.7--19.

Weeks, J.R. (2005). "Population: An Introduction to Concepts and Issues." Wadsworth.

Weida, W.J. (2001). *A Review of the Proposal and Draft DEQ Permit for A Farrow-to-Finish Hog Operation By Big Sky Farms, LLC In Cassia County, Idaho*. The Global Resource Action Center for the Environment (GRACE) Factory Farm Project. www.factoryfarm.org.

21 Century Workforce Commission, 2000. *A Nation of Opportunity: Building America's 21st Century Workforce.* Washington D.C.

Zhang, T. (2007a). "Age and Elderly Entrepreneurship," *Working Paper*, George Mason University, Fairfax, Virginia.

Zhang, T. (2007b). "Social and Policy Factors for Elderly Entrepreneurship," *Working Paper*, George Mason University, Fairfax, Virginia.

Zhang, T. (2007c). "The Role of Elderly Entrepreneurship in Metropolitan Economy," *Working Paper*, George Mason University, Fairfax, Virginia.

Zhang, T. (2007d). "Labor and Fiscal Impact of Elderly Entrepreneurship," *Working Paper*, George Mason University, Fairfax, Virginia.

Zhang, T. (2008). *Elderly Entrepreneurship in an Aging U.S. Economy: It's Never Too Late*, London, New Jersey, Singapore: World Scientific.

Appendices

Appendix 3.1 Age Pyramids of U.S. Population from 1975 through 2050

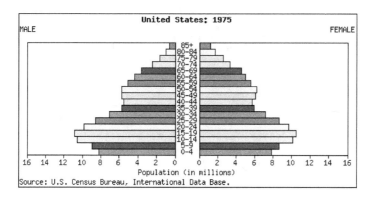

Age Pyramid of the United States in 1975

Source: Zhang (2008).

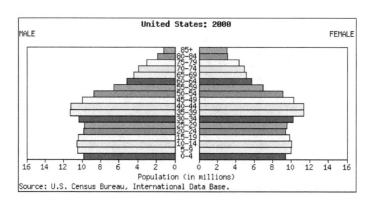

Age Pyramid of the United States in 2000

Source: Zhang (2008).

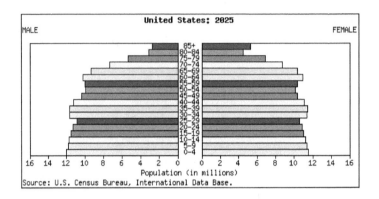

Age Pyramid of the United States in 2025

Source: Zhang (2008).

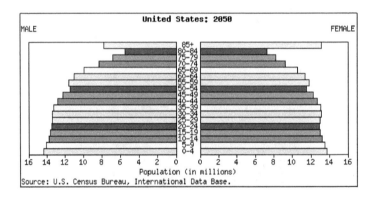

Age Pyramid of the United States in 2050

Source: Zhang (2008).

Appendix 4.1 Labor force status among the elderly

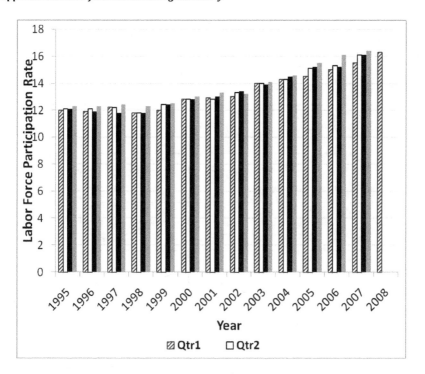

Civilian Labor Force Participation Rate for Older Americans (Aged 65 and over), 1994 - 2005

Source: U.S. Department of Labor, Bureau of Labor Statistics 1994-2005

Appendix 7.1 Classes of Workers for All People Aged 16 and above, 2000

Cohorts	Not Employed	Self - Employed	Unemployed	Private Sector employee	Government employees	Unpaid Family Workers	Total
Younger	20162559	13357946	945867	118000000	22686759	515749	176000000
Row %	11.46	7.59	0.54	67.22	12.9	0.29	100
Column %	42.03	84.55	88.16	93.24	91.46	77.26	81.02
Older	27810597	2440250	127,025	8566917	2118136	151,832	41214757
Row %	67.48	5.92	0.31	20.79	5.14	0.37	100
Column %	57.97	15.45	11.84	6.76	8.54	22.74	18.98
Total	47973156	15798196	1072892	127000000	24804895	667,581	217000000
Row %	22.09	7.28	0.49	58.41	11.42	0.31	100
Column %	100	100	100	100	100	100	100

Source: Zhang (2008).

Appendix 7.2 Self-employment, Wage-and-salary Employment, Unemployment, Total Employment, Labor Force, and Population

Age	Self-employed	Wage-and-salary Employment	Unemployment	Total Employment	Labor Force	Population
16	45352	1681117	116039	1747936	1863975	3899205
17	46916	2427231	96128	2493893	2590021	3988247
18	55318	3106890	73951	3183793	3257744	4036325
19	63457	3412033	57221	3498076	3555297	4020860
20	83849	3568326	39942	3668584	3708526	4053266
21	88119	3395423	31255	3495932	3527187	3809200
22	92691	3409627	25017	3515243	3540260	3791971
23	99390	3315858	25207	3425182	3450389	3687242
24	113412	3324468	20325	3446811	3467136	3700946
25	138779	3234404	15846	3383649	3399495	3641692
26	149140	3154679	17428	3312488	3329916	3550583
27	174336	3344456	18633	3525534	3544167	3789587
28	188922	3503597	16456	3700949	3717405	3970766
29	234851	3708224	15618	3950608	3966226	4231340
30	252826	3631464	12260	3893919	3906179	4176413
31	248831	3404087	14768	3662788	3677556	3948639
32	266307	3410770	15700	3685415	3701115	3983560
33	289593	3401496	12191	3699507	3711698	4005975
34	314591	3510076	14375	3835063	3849438	4169227
35	371021	3831086	12136	4212779	4224915	4594137
36	375298	3800006	16769	4184972	4201741	4576330
37	415752	3735128	14721	4165716	4180437	4557604
38	419068	3832385	17668	4263462	4281130	4667336
39	451441	3815744	18782	4278541	4297323	4700993
40	449183	3878915	18058	4340124	4358182	4781170
41	439721	3697270	15458	4150884	4166342	4547057
42	470418	3706206	12359	4189581	4201940	4597719
43	443935	3649730	14981	4103364	4118345	4506364
44	452253	3549431	14274	4011134	4025408	4412285
45	460972	3481200	15268	3952662	3967930	4361755
46	431065	3276448	14597	3718575	3733172	4117379
47	429905	3175899	12816	3616493	3629309	4022054

48	425099	3108406	12121	3544398	3556519	3935008
49	413657	2986082	10227	3409170	3419397	3817812
50	401574	2876985	10064	3288672	3298736	3713704
51	395148	2792147	10473	3198050	3208523	3622432
52	413181	2806089	9658	3227589	3237247	3676268
53	401117	2768036	9678	3181390	3191068	3641443
54	324068	2067676	8808	2401406	2410214	2798971
55	319127	2014947	5972	2343415	2349387	2797922
56	329718	1995961	8191	2333941	2342132	2798112
57	331252	1988685	7894	2328677	2336571	2830211
58	289623	1735051	5596	2034603	2040199	2534908
59	263225	1564672	4487	1836386	1840873	2350471
60	252044	1479352	3718	1740950	1744668	2287353
61	242401	1379738	2733	1628892	1631625	2217780
62	227749	1294914	4023	1531047	1535070	2185994
63	207091	1161451	3594	1379040	1382634	2046326
64	194851	1091338	3181	1294463	1297644	2039034
65	174459	811172	5054	994685	999739	1867219
66	152020	724350	3551	885420	888971	1784044
67	151016	647098	4884	806963	811847	1844288
68	134086	594722	4233	738881	743114	1839990
69	132834	582608	3300	724214	727514	1904599
70	125723	530578	3540	665176	668716	1933542
71	116417	443898	4318	567058	571376	1828967
72	111680	396954	5052	514899	519951	1801142
73	93516	336548	2405	435788	438193	1720648
74	83154	298507	4857	387223	392080	1660905
75	76079	257784	4111	339654	343765	1583102
76	71409	225040	3255	301329	304584	1511168
77	59387	196630	3523	260570	264093	1449481
78	53092	175275	4020	231930	235950	1387411
79	43778	154159	3286	201901	205187	1310681
80	45931	124421	5491	174412	179903	1234505
81	32373	105453	3697	139954	143651	1116593
82	29472	91682	3702	123547	127249	1028497
83	21890	77738	4962	103158	108120	936248

84	23807	65792	2870	91691	94561	833116
85	19110	60255	4851	80973	85824	787926
86	12082	47406	4071	60623	64694	664916
87	11962	42392	4367	55326	59693	597054
88	10320	34915	3085	46932	50017	499614
89	6449	28011	2698	35463	38161	421775
92	1504	5492	76	7032	7108	75810
93	17009	78430	16968	97743	114711	1319414

Source: Zhang (2008).

Appendix 7.3 Self-employment Rates by Age

Age	In Total Employment	In Labor Force	In Total Population
16	2.594603006	2.433079843	1.16310889
17	1.881235482	1.811413884	1.176356429
18	1.73748733	1.698046255	1.37050411
19	1.814054354	1.784857918	1.578194715
20	2.28559575	2.26097916	2.068677457
21	2.52061539	2.498279791	2.313320382
22	2.636830512	2.618197534	2.444401605
23	2.901743615	2.880544773	2.695510628
24	3.290345772	3.271057149	3.064405695
25	4.101459696	4.082341642	3.810838478
26	4.502355933	4.478791657	4.200436942
27	4.94495302	4.918955568	4.600395769
28	5.104690716	5.082093557	4.757822546
29	5.944679907	5.921271254	5.550274854
30	6.492841787	6.472463243	6.053663754
31	6.793486273	6.7662056	6.301690279
32	7.225970481	7.195318168	6.68515097
33	7.82788085	7.802170327	7.229026641
34	8.203020394	8.172387762	7.545547412

207

35	8.807036875	8.781738804	8.07596726
36	8.967754145	8.931964155	8.2008509
37	9.980325111	9.945180372	9.122161557
38	9.829288968	9.788724005	8.978740763
39	10.55128372	10.50516798	9.60309875
40	10.34954301	10.30665998	9.394834319
41	10.59343022	10.55412638	9.670452779
42	11.22828273	11.19525743	10.23155178
43	10.81880623	10.77945145	9.851290309
44	11.2749412	11.23496053	10.2498592
45	11.6623177	11.61744285	10.56849823
46	11.59220938	11.54688292	10.46940299
47	11.88734501	11.84536781	10.68869289
48	11.99354587	11.95267057	10.80300218
49	12.13365717	12.09736687	10.83492325
50	12.21082552	12.17357194	10.81330122
51	12.35590438	12.31557324	10.90836212
52	12.801537	12.7633449	11.23914252
53	12.60823099	12.56999224	11.01533101
54	13.49492755	13.44561105	11.5781121
55	13.6180318	13.58341559	11.40585763
56	14.12709233	14.07768648	11.78358836
57	14.22490109	14.1768429	11.70414503
58	14.23486547	14.19582109	11.42538506
59	14.33386009	14.2989223	11.1988193
60	14.47738304	14.4465308	11.01902505
61	14.88134266	14.85641615	10.92989386
62	14.87537613	14.83639183	10.41855559
63	15.01704084	14.97800575	10.12013726
64	15.05265118	15.01575162	9.556044676
65	17.53912043	17.45045457	9.343253255
66	17.16925301	17.10067033	8.521090287
67	18.714117	18.60153453	8.188308984
68	18.1471712	18.04379947	7.287322214
69	18.34181609	18.2586177	6.974381484

70	18.90071199	18.80065678	6.502212003
71	20.5299987	20.37484949	6.365177721
72	21.6896906	21.47894705	6.200510565
73	21.45905807	21.34128112	5.434929166
74	21.47444754	21.20842685	5.006547635
75	22.39897072	22.13110701	4.805691611
76	23.69801778	23.44476401	4.72541769
77	22.79118855	22.48715415	4.097121659
78	22.89138964	22.50137741	3.826695911
79	21.682904	21.33565967	3.340095721
80	26.33477054	25.53098058	3.720600565
81	23.13117167	22.53586818	2.899265892
82	23.85488923	23.16088928	2.865540687
83	21.21987631	20.24602294	2.338055729
84	25.96438036	25.1763412	2.857585258
85	23.60045941	22.26649888	2.425354665
86	19.92972964	18.67561134	1.81707163
87	21.62093771	20.03920058	2.003503871
88	21.98926106	20.63298479	2.065594639
89	18.18515072	16.89945232	1.529014285
92	21.38794084	21.15925718	1.983907136
93	17.40175767	14.82769743	1.289132903

Source: Zhang (2008).

Appendix 7.4 Self-employment Rates vs. Wage-and-salary Employment Rates in Labor Force by Age

Age	Self-employed	Wage-and-Salary Employment	Unemployed
16	2.433079843	90.18988989	6.225351735
17	1.811413884	93.71472278	3.711475698
18	1.698046255	95.36937218	2.270006483
19	1.784857918	95.97040697	1.609457663
20	2.26097916	96.21952226	1.077031683
21	2.498279791	96.26433189	0.886116897

209

22	2.618197534	96.31007327	0.706643015
23	2.880544773	96.10099035	0.730555308
24	3.271057149	95.88513401	0.586218712
25	4.082341642	95.14366104	0.466128057
26	4.478791657	94.73749488	0.523376566
27	4.918955568	94.3650793	0.525737077
28	5.082093557	94.24846096	0.442674392
29	5.921271254	93.49502525	0.393774838
30	6.472463243	92.96716817	0.313861705
31	6.7662056	92.56383859	0.401571043
32	7.195318168	92.15520188	0.424196492
33	7.802170327	91.64258515	0.328448058
34	8.172387762	91.18411571	0.373431135
35	8.781738804	90.67841602	0.287248383
36	8.931964155	90.43884428	0.39909647
37	9.945180372	89.34778828	0.352140219
38	9.788724005	89.51807116	0.412694779
39	10.50516798	88.79351168	0.437062795
40	10.30665998	89.00305219	0.414347083
41	10.55412638	88.74139473	0.37102091
42	11.19525743	88.20225896	0.294126047
43	10.77945145	88.62127869	0.363762628
44	11.23496053	88.17568306	0.354597596
45	11.61744285	87.73340255	0.384785014
46	11.54688292	87.76579274	0.391007969
47	11.84536781	87.50698824	0.353125071
48	11.95267057	87.40023602	0.340810776
49	12.09736687	87.32773644	0.299087822
50	12.17357194	87.21476954	0.305086554
51	12.31557324	87.02281392	0.326411872
52	12.7633449	86.68133757	0.298339917
53	12.56999224	86.74324709	0.303284042
54	13.44561105	85.78806695	0.365444728
55	13.58341559	85.76479737	0.254193966
56	14.07768648	85.21983389	0.349724098
57	14.1768429	85.11125919	0.337845501

58	14.19582109	85.04322372	0.274286969
59	14.2989223	84.99619474	0.24374305
60	14.4465308	84.7927514	0.213106448
61	14.85641615	84.56220026	0.167501724
62	14.83639183	84.35537142	0.262072739
63	14.97800575	84.0027802	0.259938639
64	15.01575162	84.10149471	0.245136571
65	17.45045457	81.13837712	0.505531944
66	17.10067033	81.48184811	0.399450601
67	18.60153453	79.70689058	0.601591187
68	18.04379947	80.03105849	0.569629963
69	18.2586177	80.08203279	0.453599518
70	18.80065678	79.34280023	0.529372708
71	20.37484949	77.68929742	0.755719526
72	21.47894705	76.34450169	0.971630019
73	21.34128112	76.80360024	0.548844915
74	21.20842685	76.1342073	1.2387778
75	22.13110701	74.98843687	1.195875089
76	23.44476401	73.88438001	1.068670712
77	22.48715415	74.4548322	1.333999765
78	22.50137741	74.2848061	1.703750795
79	21.33565967	75.13097808	1.60146598
80	25.53098058	69.16004736	3.052200352
81	22.53586818	73.40916527	2.573598513
82	23.16088928	72.04928919	2.909256654
83	20.24602294	71.89974103	4.589345172
84	25.1763412	69.57625237	3.035077886
85	22.26649888	70.20763423	5.652265101
86	18.67561134	73.27727455	6.292701023
87	20.03920058	71.01670213	7.315765668
88	20.63298479	69.80626587	6.167902913
89	16.89945232	73.40216451	7.070045334
92	21.15925718	77.26505346	1.069217783
93	14.82769743	68.37182136	14.79195544

Source: Zhang (2008).

Appendix 7.5 Older vs. Younger Knowledge-Based Self-employment Rate

	Younger workers			Older workers		
	Non self-employed	Self-employed	Total	Non self-employed	Self-employed	Total
Non-knowledge-based	98359877	7721201	106100000	7978453	1194935	9E+06
	92.72	7.28	100.00	86.97	13.03	100
	69.07	57.8	68.11	72.77	48.97	68.44
Knowledge-based	44039240	5636745	49675985	2985457	1245315	4E+06
	88.65	11.35	100.00	70.57	29.43	100
	30.93	**42.2**	31.89	27.23	**51.03**	31.56
Total	1.42E+08	13357946	155800000	10963910	2440250	1E+07
	91.42	8.58	100.00	81.79	18.21	100
	100	100	100	100	100	100

(For younger) Pearson chi2(1) = 7.1e+05   Pr = 0.000,

(for older) Pearson chi2(1) = 5.2e+05   Pr = 0.000.

Source: Zhang (2008).

Appendix 7.6 Summary of Variables

Variable	Definition	Data type	Source	Unit of analysis
Dependent variable				
Entrepreneurs (or creative class self-employed)	Value of 1: creative class self-employed; value of 0: all other people participating in employment	Dummy	PUMS	Individual
Independent variables				
Key variable under investigation				
Old age	Value of 0: for age 16-61, value of 1: for age 62+	Dummy	PUMS	Individual

Human capital variable

Education	The higher value, the higher education attainment by degree or level individuals have achieved	Categorical	PUMS	Individual
Employment Disability	Value of 0: no disability; value of 1: with employment disability	Dummy	PUMS	Individual

Demographic characteristics

Widowed	0: not, 1: widowed	Dummy	PUMS	Individual
Divorced	0: not; 1: divorced	Dummy	PUMS	Individual
Married	0: not; 1: currently married and live with spouse	Dummy	PUMS	Individual
Single	0: not; 1: never married	Dummy	PUMS	Individual
White	0: not; 1: race is white	Dummy	PUMS	Individual
Black	0: not; 1: race is black	Dummy	PUMS	Individual
Asian	0: not; 1: race is Asian and pacific islander	Dummy	PUMS	Individual
Mixed	0: not; 1: mixed race	Dummy	PUMS	Individual
Male	0: female; 1: male	Dummy	PUMS	Individual

Responsibility for grandchildren

Responsibility for grandchild	The higher value, having had more years of responsibility for grandchildren	Categorical	PUMS	Individual

Immigration status

Year to U.S.	The value labels the year of entering. The higher value, the later entering the U.S.	Categorical	PUMS	Individual

Wealth

Property value	Increase with value	Categorical	PUMS	Individual
Household income	Increase with value	Categorical	PUMS	Individual

Sampling weight

Weight	Sampling weight calculated by PUMS	Numerical	PUMS	Individual

Source: Zhang (2008).

213

Appendix 7.7 Logit Model Results for Older Age Effect on Entrepreneurship in 2000

	Coef.	Std. Err.	P>|z|	[95% Conf.Interval]	
Dependent variable					
Probability of being an entrepreneur					
Logit model estimation: coefficients of independent variables					
Key variable under investigation					
Being a senior	*0.8293655*	0.0011266	*0.0000*	0.8271573	0.8315737
Human capital					
Education	0.1627496	0.0001764	0.0000	0.1624038	0.1630953
Employment Disability	0.0856348	0.0013727	0.0000	0.0829443	0.0883253
Immigration status					
Year to the U.S.	0.0000551	7.10E-07	0.0000	0.0000537	0.0000565
Demographic characteristics					
Widowed	0.1337199	0.004247	0.0000	0.1253959	0.1420439
Divorced	0.1048729	0.0036532	0.0000	0.0977127	0.1120331
Married	0.0664935	0.0034734	0.0000	0.0596857	0.0733012
Not Married	-0.6025368	0.0036137	0.0000	-0.6096195	-0.595454
White	0.5684632	0.0029441	0.0000	0.5626929	0.5742336
Black	-0.331745	0.0036106	0.0000	-0.3388218	-0.3246683
Asian	0.4833203	0.0034542	0.0000	0.4765502	0.4900904
Mixed	0.4255401	0.0042629	0.0000	0.4171851	0.4338952
Male	0.7842681	0.0008722	0.0000	0.7825587	0.7859776
Responsibility for grandchildren					
Responsibility for grandchildren	-0.0525849	0.0013121	0.0000	-0.0551566	-0.0500132
Wealth					
Household income	2.54E-06	4.65E-09	0.0000	2.54E-06	2.55E-06
Property value	0.04619	0.0000683	0.0000	0.0460561	0.0463239
Constant					
Constant	-6.692379	.0047471	-0.0000	-6.701683	-6.683075
Other statistics					
Number of observations			168088331		
LR chi2(16)			6471557.54		
Prob > chi2			0.0000		

214

Pseudo R2	0.1126
Log likelihood	-25495547

Source: Zhang (2008).

Appendix 8.1 Residual Map of Sampled MSA / PMSA

Source: Zhang (2008).

Appendix 8.2 Summary of the Variables

Variable	Obs	Mean	Std. Dev.	Min	Max
log(Y/L)	90	10.178960	0.141213	9.679580	10.611000
logK	90	12.067890	0.272218	11.400330	12.827560
LogR	90	11.003620	0.925877	9.361859	13.457320
LogE	-90	-3.959908	0.315392	-5.003359	-3.303833
Log(eld. E)	-90	-3.666309	0.317785	-5.28401 -	-3.085954

215

	Obs				
log(yng. E)	-90	-3.530132	0.220013	-4.137795	-2.955097

Source: Zhang (2008).

Appendix 8.3 Description of all Variables Used in the Path Analysis

Variable	Obs	Mean	Std. Dev.	Min	Max
Log(Social Security fund contribution)	52	15.5349	1.069531	13.56903	17.8756
Log(Employment)	51	13.83485	1.022344	11.99076	16.04343
Wage-and-salary employment share	51	87.16148	2.64617	79.66628	91.3447
Elderly entrepreneurs	51	19948.47	21870.16	1294	126732

Source: Zhang (2008).

Appendix 8.4 Pearson Correlation Matrix

		Log (Social Security Contribution)	Log (Employment)	% Wage-and-salary employment among Total Employment	# of Elderly entrepreneurs
Log (Social Security Contribution)	Corr.	1	-	-	-
	Sig. (p)	-	-	-	-
	Obs.	51	-	-	-
Log (Employment)	Corr.	0.9913	1	-	-
	Sig. (p)	0.0000	-	-	-
	Obs.	51	51	-	-
% Wage-and-salary employment among Total Employment	Corr.	0.4605	0.4151	1	-
	Sig. (p)	0.0007	0.0025	-	-
	Obs.	51	51	51	
# of Elderly entrepreneurs	Corr.	**0.7768**	**0.7854**	0.0906	1
	Sig. (p)	0.0000	0.0000	0.5273	-

	Obs.	51	51	51	51

Appendix 8.5 OLS Results—Dependent Variable: SOCIAL SECURITY FUND CONTRIBUTION (IN LOG)

REGRESSION

SUMMARY OF OUTPUT: ORDINARY LEAST SQUARES ESTIMATION

```
Data set            : ss test 8
Dependent Variable  :   LNSSCTBSD   Number of Observations:    51
Mean dependent var  :9.80392e-008  Number of Variables   :     4
S.D. dependent var  :   0.990148   Degrees of Freedom    :    47


R-squared           :   0.986071   F-statistic           :    1109.05
Adjusted R-squared  :   0.985181   Prob(F-statistic)     :1.33137e-043
Sum squared residual:   0.696474   Log likelihood        :    37.1197
Sigma-square        :   0.0148186  Akaike info criterion :   -66.2394
S.E. of regression  :   0.121732   Schwarz criterion     :   -58.5121
Sigma-square ML     :   0.0136563
S.E of regression ML:   0.11686
```

Variable	Coefficient	Std.Error	t-Statistic	Probability
CONSTANT	1.071848e-007	0.01704584	6.288036e-006	1.0000000
LNEMPLYSD	0.9318842	0.0335118	27.80765	0.0000000
WSEMPLYSD	0.07011949	0.0208303	3.366226	0.0015266
ELDESD	0.03860968	0.03061392	1.26118	0.2134679

REGRESSION DIAGNOSTICS

```
MULTICOLLINEARITY CONDITION NUMBER    3.625069
TEST ON NORMALITY OF ERRORS
TEST                 DF        VALUE          PROB
Jarque-Bera          2         0.5248993      0.7691651
```

DIAGNOSTICS FOR HETEROSKEDASTICITY

217

```
RANDOM COEFFICIENTS
TEST                      DF          VALUE           PROB
Breusch-Pagan test        3           2.886281        0.4094928
Koenker-Bassett test      3           3.79142         0.2848857
SPECIFICATION ROBUST TEST
TEST                      DF          VALUE           PROB
White                     9           10.63702        0.3014118
```

DIAGNOSTICS FOR SPATIAL DEPENDENCE

```
FOR WEIGHT MATRIX : state2.GAL  (row-standardized weights)
TEST                            MI/DF      VALUE        PROB
Moran's I (error)               0.419750   4.9292894    0.0000008
Lagrange Multiplier (lag)       1          0.2062607    0.6497141
Robust LM (lag)                 1          1.6456109    0.1995574
Lagrange Multiplier (error)     1          18.6461301   0.0000157
Robust LM (error)               1          20.0854802   0.0000074
Lagrange Multiplier (SARMA)     2          20.2917410   0.0000392
========================= END OF REPORT =============================
```

Source: Zhang(2008).

Appendix 8.6 Spatial Error Model—Dependent Variable: SOCIAL SECURITY FUND CONTRIBUTION (IN LOG)

REGRESSION

SUMMARY OF OUTPUT: SPATIAL ERROR MODEL - MAXIMUM LIKELIHOOD ESTIMATION

```
Data set            : ss test 8
Spatial Weight      : state2.GAL
Dependent Variable  :  LNSSCTBSD  Number of Observations:   51
Mean dependent var  :   0.000000  Number of Variables   :    4
S.D. dependent var  :   0.990148  Degree of Freedom     :   47
Lag coeff. (Lambda) :   0.711461


R-squared           :   0.991881  R-squared (BUSE)      : -
Sq. Correlation     : -           Log likelihood        :   46.927040
Sigma-square        :   0.007960  Akaike info criterion :   -85.8541
S.E of regression   :   0.0892187 Schwarz criterion     :   -78.126778
```

```
Variable    Coefficient    Std.Error    z-value        Probability
------------------------------------------------------------------------
CONSTANT    0.03346457     0.03722525   0.8989751      0.3686659
LNEMPLYSD   0.9824113      0.02342698   41.93504       0.0000000
WSEMPLYSD   0.05506256     0.01873747   2.938634       0.0032968
ELDESD      0.01558146     0.0202569    0.7691927      0.4417788
LAMBDA      0.7114615      0.1019393    6.979263       0.0000000
------------------------------------------------------------------------
```

REGRESSION DIAGNOSTICS

DIAGNOSTICS FOR HETEROSKEDASTICITY

RANDOM COEFFICIENTS

TEST	DF	VALUE	PROB
Breusch-Pagan test	3	1.326521	0.7228453

DIAGNOSTICS FOR SPATIAL DEPENDENCE

SPATIAL ERROR DEPENDENCE FOR WEIGHT MATRIX : **state2.GAL**

TEST	DF	VALUE	PROB
Likelihood Ratio Test	1	19.61471	**0.0000095**

```
========================= END OF REPORT =============================
```
Source: Zhang(2008).

Appendix 8.7 OLS Results—Dependent Variable: EMPLOYMENT SIZE (IN LOG)

REGRESSION2

SUMMARY OF OUTPUT: ORDINARY LEAST SQUARES ESTIMATION

```
Data set            : ss test 8
Dependent Variable  :  LNEMPLYSD  Number of Observations:  51
Mean dependent var  :-2.61229e-017  Number of Variables   :   3
S.D. dependent var  :  0.990148  Degrees of Freedom    :  48

R-squared           :  0.736099  F-statistic           :    66.9431
Adjusted R-squared  :  0.725103  Prob(F-statistic)     :1.30195e-014
Sum squared residual:  13.1951   Log likelihood        :   -37.8903
Sigma-square        :  0.274897  Akaike info criterion :    81.7806
S.E. of regression  :  0.524306  Schwarz criterion     :    87.5761
Sigma-square ML     :  0.258727
S.E of regression ML:  0.508652
```

219

```
-----------------------------------------------------------------------
    Variable     Coefficient     Std.Error    t-Statistic    Probability
-----------------------------------------------------------------------
    CONSTANT   7.835138e-008    0.07341757   1.067202e-006  1.0000000
   WSEMPLYSD     0.3468118      0.07445423    4.658053      0.0000256
     ELDESD      0.7539539      0.07445423   10.12641       0.0000000
-----------------------------------------------------------------------
```

REGRESSION DIAGNOSTICS

MULTICOLLINEARITY CONDITION NUMBER   1.095091

TEST ON NORMALITY OF ERRORS

TEST	DF	VALUE	PROB
Jarque-Bera	2	17.52881	*0.0001562*

DIAGNOSTICS FOR HETEROSKEDASTICITY

RANDOM COEFFICIENTS

TEST	DF	VALUE	PROB
Breusch-Pagan test	2	16.35471	*0.0002809*
Koenker-Bassett test	2	10.19105	*0.0061241*

SPECIFICATION ROBUST TEST

TEST	DF	VALUE	PROB
White	5	28.66795	*0.0000269*

DIAGNOSTICS FOR SPATIAL DEPENDENCE

FOR WEIGHT MATRIX : **state2.GAL**   (row-standardized weights)

TEST	MI/DF	VALUE	PROB
Moran's I (error)	-0.036353	-0.0700213	0.9441766
Lagrange Multiplier (lag)	1	0.3297148	0.5658271
Robust LM (lag)	1	1.3991996	0.2368577
Lagrange Multiplier (error)	1	0.1398548	0.7084254
Robust LM (error)	1	1.2093396	0.2714630
Lagrange Multiplier (SARMA)	2	1.5390544	0.4632320

```
======================== END OF REPORT ============================
```

Source: Zhang(2008).

Appendix 8.8 OLS Results—Dependent Variable: WAGE-AND-SALARY EMPLOYMENT SHARE

REGRESSION3

SUMMARY OF OUTPUT: ORDINARY LEAST SQUARES ESTIMATION

Data set   : **ss test 8**
Dependent Variable   : **WSEMPLYSD** Number of Observations: 51
Mean dependent var   :-9.80392e-008 Number of Variables   :   2
S.D. dependent var   :   0.990148 Degrees of Freedom   :   49

R-squared   :   0.008206 F-statistic   :   0.405431
Adjusted R-squared   : *-0.012034* Prob(F-statistic)   :   0.527262
Sum squared residual: 49.5897 Log likelihood   : -71.6508
Sigma-square   :   1.01203 Akaike info criterion :   147.302
S.E. of regression   :   1.006 Schwarz criterion   :   151.165
Sigma-square ML   :   0.972347
S.E of regression ML: 0.986077

Variable	Coefficient	Std.Error	t-Statistic	Probability
CONSTANT	-9.271051e-008	0.1408681	-6.581371e-007	1.0000000
ELDESD	0.09058805	0.1422698	0.6367343	0.5272617

REGRESSION DIAGNOSTICS

MULTICOLLINEARITY CONDITION NUMBER   1

                                (Extreme Multicollinearity)

TEST ON NORMALITY OF ERRORS

TEST	DF	VALUE	PROB
Jarque-Bera	2	8.074578	0.0176452

DIAGNOSTICS FOR HETEROSKEDASTICITY

RANDOM COEFFICIENTS

TEST	DF	VALUE	PROB
Breusch-Pagan test	1	0.06844044	0.7936212
Koenker-Bassett test	1	0.05493566	0.8146872

SPECIFICATION ROBUST TEST

TEST	DF	VALUE	PROB
White	2	5.670406	0.0587066

DIAGNOSTICS FOR SPATIAL DEPENDENCE

FOR WEIGHT MATRIX : **state2.GAL** (row-standardized weights)

221

```
TEST                            MI/DF      VALUE          PROB
Moran's I (error)             0.514850    5.7229256     0.0000000
Lagrange Multiplier (lag)          1     29.2423817    0.0000001
Robust LM (lag)                    1      6.0689888    0.0137576
Lagrange Multiplier (error)        1     28.0522600    0.0000001
Robust LM (error)                  1      4.8788671    0.0271875
Lagrange Multiplier (SARMA)        2     34.1212488    0.0000000
========================= END OF REPORT =============================
```

Source: Zhang (2008).

***Appendix 8.9 Spatial Lag Model—Dependent Variable: WAGE-AND-SALARY EMPLOYMENT
SHARE***

REGRESSION3

SUMMARY OF OUTPUT: SPATIAL LAG MODEL - MAXIMUM LIKELIHOOD ESTIMATION

```
Data set          : ss test 8
Spatial Weight    : state2.GAL
Dependent Variable :   WSEMPLYSD  Number of Observations:   51
Mean dependent var :-9.80392e-008  Number of Variables  :    3
S.D. dependent var :   0.990148  Degrees of Freedom    :   48
Lag coeff.  (Rho) :   0.697242

R-squared         :   0.473004  Log likelihood        :  -59.2797
Sq. Correlation   : -           Akaike info criterion :   124.559
Sigma-square      :   0.516663  Schwarz criterion     :   130.355
S.E of regression :   0.718793
```

Variable	Coefficient	Std.Error	z-value	Probability
W_WSEMPLYSD	0.6972425	0.1053229	6.620043	**0.0000000**
CONSTANT	0.001568446	0.1006529	0.01558271	0.9875672
ELDESD	0.01681775	0.1016528	0.165443	0.8685953

REGRESSION DIAGNOSTICS

DIAGNOSTICS FOR HETEROSKEDASTICITY

```
RANDOM COEFFICIENTS
TEST                                    DF      VALUE           PROB
Breusch-Pagan test                      1    0.0007422072      0.9782655

DIAGNOSTICS FOR SPATIAL DEPENDENCE
SPATIAL LAG DEPENDENCE FOR WEIGHT MATRIX : state2.GAL
TEST                                    DF      VALUE           PROB
Likelihood Ratio Test                   1     24.74209         0.0000007
========================= END OF REPORT ==============================
```

Source: Zhang(2008).

Appendix 9.1 Major ATIS Deployments

Source: Gilroy et al, 1998.

Appendix 9.2 Older Drivers Experience the Following Physical and Mental Capacity Changes

* Declining vision and visual field cognition

* Slowed decision making

* Slowed perception reaction time

Source: Federal Highway Administration, 1998

Appendix 9.3 Cross tabulation for Private Owned Vehicle and Transit Usage among Older vs. Younger Travelers.

```
        Total |
        Daily |  Age of Respondent
        Trips |  Younger     Older |     Total
-----------+-----------------------+----------
        0 |     5,653     1,639 |     7,292
          |     77.52     22.48 |    100.00
          |     17.47     28.68 |     19.15
-----------+-----------------------+----------
        1 |       969        69 |     1,038
          |     93.35      6.65 |    100.00
          |      2.99      1.21 |      2.73
-----------+-----------------------+----------
        2 |     6,896     1,064 |     7,960
          |     86.63     13.37 |    100.00
          |     21.31     18.62 |     20.90
-----------+-----------------------+----------
        3 |     3,424       561 |     3,985
          |     85.92     14.08 |    100.00
          |     10.58      9.82 |     10.47
-----------+-----------------------+----------
        4 |     4,977       770 |     5,747
          |     86.60     13.40 |    100.00
          |     15.38     13.48 |     15.09
```

224

```
-----------+---------------------+----------
        5 |      3,041      486 |      3,527
          |      86.22    13.78 |     100.00
          |       9.40     8.51 |       9.26
-----------+---------------------+----------
        6 |      2,543      443 |      2,986
          |      85.16    14.84 |     100.00
          |       7.86     7.75 |       7.84
-----------+---------------------+----------
        7 |      1,636      302 |      1,938
          |      84.42    15.58 |     100.00
          |       5.05     5.29 |       5.09
-----------+---------------------+----------
        8 |      1,263      167 |      1,430
          |      88.32    11.68 |     100.00
          |       3.90     2.92 |       3.76
-----------+---------------------+----------
        9 |        752       90 |        842
          |      89.31    10.69 |     100.00
          |       2.32     1.58 |       2.21
-----------+---------------------+----------
       10 |        490       44 |        534
          |      91.76     8.24 |     100.00
          |       1.51     0.77 |       1.40
-----------+---------------------+----------
       11 |        280       30 |        310
          |      90.32     9.68 |     100.00
          |       0.87     0.53 |       0.81
-----------+---------------------+----------
       12 |        181       18 |        199
          |      90.95     9.05 |     100.00
          |       0.56     0.32 |       0.52
-----------+---------------------+----------
       13 |         96       10 |        106
          |      90.57     9.43 |     100.00
          |       0.30     0.18 |       0.28
-----------+---------------------+----------
       14 |         67        9 |         76
```

```
           |     88.16      11.84 |    100.00
           |      0.21       0.16 |      0.20
-----------+----------------------+----------
        15 |        31          7 |        38
           |     81.58      18.42 |    100.00
           |      0.10       0.12 |      0.10
-----------+----------------------+----------
        16 |        22          3 |        25
           |     88.00      12.00 |    100.00
           |      0.07       0.05 |      0.07
-----------+----------------------+----------
        17 |        20          1 |        21
           |     95.24       4.76 |    100.00
           |      0.06       0.02 |      0.06
-----------+----------------------+----------
        18 |         7          0 |         7
           |    100.00       0.00 |    100.00
           |      0.02       0.00 |      0.02
-----------+----------------------+----------
        19 |         9          1 |        10
           |     90.00      10.00 |    100.00
           |      0.03       0.02 |      0.03
-----------+----------------------+----------
        20 |         4          0 |         4
           |    100.00       0.00 |    100.00
           |      0.01       0.00 |      0.01
-----------+----------------------+----------
        22 |         1          0 |         1
           |    100.00       0.00 |    100.00
           |      0.00       0.00 |      0.00
-----------+----------------------+----------
        23 |         1          0 |        .1
           |    100.00       0.00 |    100.00
           |      0.00       0.00 |      0.00
-----------+----------------------+----------
        30 |         1          0 |         1
           |    100.00       0.00 |    100.00
           |      0.00       0.00 |      0.00
```

```
----------+----------------------+----------
   Total |    32,364      5,714 |   38,078
         |     84.99      15.01 |   100.00
         |    100.00     100.00 |   100.00


         Pearson chi2(23) = 476.2234   Pr = 0.000




   Total |
   Daily |
   Trips- | Age of Respondent
 Transit |   Younger      Older |    Total
----------+----------------------+----------
       0 |    31,577      5,625 |   37,202
         |     84.88      15.12 |   100.00
         |     97.57      98.44 |    97.70
----------+----------------------+----------
       1 |       194         21 |      215
         |     90.23       9.77 |   100.00
         |      0.60       0.37 |     0.56
----------+----------------------+----------
       2 |       481         46 |      527
         |     91.27       8.73 |   100.00
         |      1.49       0.81 |     1.38
----------+----------------------+----------
       3 |        66         13 |       79
         |     83.54      16.46 |   100.00
         |      0.20       0.23 |     0.21
----------+----------------------+----------
       4 |        28          7 |       35
         |     80.00      20.00 |   100.00
         |      0.09       0.12 |     0.09
----------+----------------------+----------
       5 |        12          0 |       12
         |    100.00       0.00 |   100.00
         |      0.04       0.00 |     0.03
----------+----------------------+----------
```

227

```
         6 |         4        1 |         5
           |     80.00    20.00 |    100.00
           |      0.01     0.02 |      0.01
-----------+--------------------+---------
         7 |         1        0 |         1
           |    100.00     0.00 |    100.00
           |      0.00     0.00 |      0.00
-----------+--------------------+---------
        10 |         1        1 |         2
           |     50.00    50.00 |    100.00
           |      0.00     0.02 |      0.01
-----------+--------------------+---------
     Total |    32,364    5,714 |    38,078
           |     84.99    15.01 |    100.00
           |    100.00   100.00 |    100.00
```

Pearson chi2(8) = 26.4160 Pr = 0.001

Appendix 9.4 Elders' Usage of Technology

Table a Familiarity with Technology

With which of the following technologies are you familiar?	
USAA-- Responses (Percentage, %)	
Internet/ World Wide Web	136 (100%)
E-mail	136 (100%)
Highway Advisory Radio	18 (13%)
Kiosk	66 (48%)
Pager	102 (74%)
Older Drivers-- Response (Percentage, %)	
Internet/ World Wide Web	117 (23%)

228

E-mail	152 (31%)
Highway Advisory Radio	87 (17%)
Kiosk	23 (5%)
Pager	64 (13%)

Source: Henk and Kuhn, 2000.

Table b Access to Technology

To which of the following do you have convenient access?	
USAA-- Responses (Percentage, %)	
Internet/ World Wide Web	133 (97%)
E-mail	132 (96%)
Computer	25 (18%)
Fax machine	74 (54%)
Pager	69 (50%)
Older Drivers-- Response (Percentage, %)	
Internet/ World Wide Web	90 (18%)
E-mail	126 (25%)
Computer	126 (25%)
Fax machine	66 (13%)
Pager	16 (3%)

Source: Henk and Kuhn, 2000.

Table c Current Use of Technology

Which methodology do you currently use to obtain information about traveler conditions, constructions, incidents, etc?	
USAA-- Responses (Percentage, %)	
Internet/ World Wide Web	44 (32%)
E-mail	9 (7%)
Television	94 (69%)
Radio	129 (94%)
Computer	20 (15%)
Older Drivers-- Response (Percentage, %)	
Internet/ World Wide Web	34 (7%)
E-mail	21 (4%)
Television	374 (75%)
Radio	343 (69%)
Computer	34 (7%)

Source: Henk and Kuhn, 2000.

www.ingramcontent.com/pod-product-compliance
Lightning Source LLC
LaVergne TN
LVHW022307060326
832902LV00020B/3328